Infrastructure and Employment Creation in the Middle East and North Africa

Infrastructure and Employment Creation in the Middle East and North Africa

Antonio Estache
Elena Ianchovichina
Robert Bacon
Ilhem Salamon

THE WORLD BANK
Washington, D.C.

Contents

Foreword   *xi*
Acknowledgments   *xiii*
About the Authors   *xv*
Abbreviations   *xvii*
Overview   *xix*

Chapter 1   **Introduction**   1
                Background Information   3
                Scope and Structure of the Study   5
                Definitions and Key Concepts   6
                References   8

Chapter 2   **The State of Employment and**
                Infrastructure and Future Needs   9
                Employment Challenges   9
                Infrastructure Endowments and Future Needs   11
                Potential of Infrastructure Investment in
                    Boosting Employment   19
                Annex 2A   Econometric Models for
                    Infrastructure Needs   23

Annex 2B   Data Sources and Descriptions Used
for Model of Investment Requirements   24
Annex 2C   Data Imputations   25
Notes   25
References   27

Chapter 3   Short-Run Employment Effects
of Infrastructure Investment   29
Techniques for Estimating the Cost of a Job and
the Employment Generated by Investment in
Infrastructure   29
Hybrid Approaches to Estimating the
Short-Term Employment Effects
of Infrastructure Investment   32
Estimating the Cost of Creating Jobs in
Oil Importing MENA Countries   35
Alternative Approaches to Estimating the
Short-Term Employment Effects of
Infrastructure Spending   45
Implications of Using Labor-Intensive
Technologies in the Maintenance of
Unpaved Roads   49
Annex 3A   Constructing Hybrid Estimates of
Employment Linked to Investment   51
Annex 3B   Estimated Shares of Inputs in
Different Types of Infrastructure   55
Annex 3C   Potential for Job Creation in the
Three Groups of MENA Countries   55
Notes   57
References   58

Chapter 4   Long-Term Employment Effects through
the Growth Channel   61
Output Elasticity with Respect to Infrastructure   62
Employment Elasticity with Respect to
Economic Output   63
Employment Elasticity with Respect to
Infrastructure   64
Long-Run Employment Response to
Infrastructure Investment   66

| | Notes | 67 |
| | References | 67 |

Chapter 5	**Policy Implications**	**69**
	Subsidized Employment Programs and Job Creation	70
	Types of Training for Lasting Job Creation	71
	Minimizing the Cost of Job Creation Targeting	73
	Is Subsidizing Job Creation a Sustainable Policy?	73
	What Are the Net Fiscal Costs and Benefits of Job Creation Programs?	76
	Concluding Remarks	77
	Notes	81
	References	82

Boxes

| 3.1 | Pros and Cons of Input-Output Table Use for Generating Employment Estimates | 33 |
| 3A.1 | Calculation of the Cost of a Type II Job Using a Hybrid Approach | 54 |

Figures

O.1	Infrastructure Needs and Financing	xxi
O.2	Cost of a Direct Job in Roads and Bridge Construction Relative to Other Sectors in 2009	xxiii
O.3	Shares of Unemployed by Education Level in Selected MENA Economies	xxvi
1.1	Public Gross Fixed Capital Formation	3
1.2	Sectors' Contribution to Annual Employment Growth in the 2000s	4
1.3	Fiscal Space Indicators	5
2.1	Labor Force Levels in MENA, 2009	11
2.2	Composition of Infrastructure Expenditure Needs by Group of Countries	17
2.3	Shares of Infrastructure and Construction Jobs in Total Employment in MENA	22
3.1	Hourly Wages as a Function of the Share of Labor Inputs in Total Costs	47

Tables

O.1   Infrastructure-Related Short-Term Job Creation   xxiii
1.1   MENA Classification   6
2.1   Employment and the Size of the Labor Force in MENA   10
2.2   Infrastructure Endowments in the Developing World   12
2.3   Infrastructure Endowments in MENA by Country Grouping   12
2.4   Unit Costs of Infrastructure by Sector   14
2.5   Roads Maintenance and Rehabilitation Program   15
2.6   Annual Expenditure Needs for Infrastructure in
        the MENA Region   16
2.7   Annual Infrastructure Investment and Maintenance Needs
        in MENA by Type of Investment as Percent of GDP   18
2.8   Expenditure Needs for Water and Sanitation in
        Urban and Rural Areas   18
2.9   Access Shortfall Compared to MDG Linear Path
        Achievement   19
2.10   Employment Shares of Infrastructure and
        Construction Sectors   20
2.11   Infrastructure Jobs by Sector in MENA   21
2C.1   Imputation of Average Investment as Percent of GDP
        When Data Were Not Available   25
3.1   Regression of Semiskilled Hourly Construction Wage on
        GDP per Capita   34
3.2   Construction Sector Hourly Wages in the
        Arab Republic of Egypt, January 2009   35
3.3   Sector Coverage Provided by Various
        Input-Output Tables   36
3.4   Cost of Creating a Job in Selected Infrastructure
        Sectors in the Arab Republic of Egypt, 2009   37
3.5   Cost of Creating Infrastructure-Related Jobs by Country 39
3.6   Estimated Costs of a Type II Job in Six MENA OICs, 2009 41
3.7   Estimated Costs of a Direct Job in Six MENA OICs, 2009 42
3.8   Number of Type II Jobs Generated per US$1 Billion of
        Spending, 2009   43
3.9   Shares of Total Investment Needs by Sector for OIC   44
3.10   Number of Type II Jobs Created by a US$1 Billion
        Portfolio of Infrastructure Spending   44
3.11   Estimated Hourly Wages in Infrastructure Works, 2010   46
3.12   Effect of US$1 Billion of Infrastructure Investment on
        Job Creation in MENA   48

3.13   Estimated Potential Job Creation in Response to
        Meeting Infrastructure Needs in MENA   49
3.14   Road Maintenance and Rehabilitation Program by
        Type of Technology   50
3.15   Investment Needs for Unpaved Road Maintenance by
        Type of Technology   51
4.1   Studies Providing Estimates of the Output Elasticity
        with Respect to Infrastructure   63
4.2   Employment Elasticities with Respect to GDP in
        MENA, 2009   64
4.3   Lower and Upper Bounds for the Employment Elasticity
        with Respect to Infrastructure   65
4.4   Employment Response to Infrastructure Investment
        Resulting in a Percentage Point Additional Growth   67

Foreword

Political transitions have lifted expectations in the Middle East and North Africa (MENA) region for rapid improvements in the population's well-being. The issue of jobs is central to well-being, but progress to date has been insufficient to address the needs of the fast-growing labor force. The transition period has been especially challenging. Since the beginning of the Arab Spring, unemployment rates have soared in many transition economies while private investment and economic growth have declined and government finances have deteriorated. Economic weakness in key European markets and the slow global economic recovery have added to domestic pressures.

Achieving tangible results relatively quickly on the jobs agenda has, therefore, become imperative in the MENA region. An important question facing governments in the region is how to stimulate employment creation in the immediate future while building foundations for sustainable growth and job creation. *Infrastructure and Employment Creation in the Middle East and North Africa* discusses how infrastructure investments can be part of the solution to this problem. The authors find the potential of infrastructure investments to create jobs to be significant, with some countries and some sectors having a much greater potential than others.

The report outlines how policy makers can make infrastructure investment an effective instrument of job creation in the face of fiscal pressures to reduce spending. Infrastructure projects will need to be prioritized based on a country's employment and infrastructure needs to boost the short-term job creation impact of public investment programs, while building the foundation for long-run growth. Importantly, strengthening governance and the efficiency of investment spending will be critical for delivering results through infrastructure investments.

Infrastructure and Employment Creation in the Middle East and North Africa offers new and compelling evidence on the potential for infrastructure investment to create jobs, while meeting country needs for better transport, communications, and housing. The authors show that, in the short-run, every US$1 billion invested in infrastructure has the potential to generate, on average, 110,000 infrastructure-related jobs in the oil importing countries; 26,000 jobs in the Gulf Cooperation Council economies; and 49,000 jobs in the developing oil exporting countries. With estimated annual infrastructure needs of about US$106 billion, the region could generate 2.5 million jobs by meeting these needs. However, these jobs would be lost if countries instead decide to trim their public investment rates going forward.

Despite these gains, infrastructure alone cannot resolve the substantial employment challenges in the region. As a complement to labor-intensive public works, subsidized employment programs combined with training and counseling can also be used to create jobs. Countries will also need to take action on a broader set of reforms aimed at generating a more dynamic private sector, by improving business regulations, promoting access to finance, and building more transparent and accountable institutions. While such reforms take time to demonstrate results, infrastructure investment can help maintain confidence, providing immediate gains on jobs and tangible improvements in the environment.

Infrastructure investment can provide a quick response, helping to build confidence by creating jobs during the transition period, while putting in place the roads, housing, utilities, and communications platforms necessary for long-run growth. We hope that the analysis and data presented on alternative types of investment across the region will be useful in helping policy makers to implement the infrastructure programs that best fit their needs.

Caroline Freund
Chief Economist
Middle East and North Africa Region

Acknowledgments

This study was prepared by a team led by Elena Ianchovichina (Lead Economist, MNACE, and principal co-author) and Ilhem Salamon (Senior Energy Economist, MNSEG, and principal co-author), and comprised Robert Bacon (principal co-author), Antonio Estache (principal co-author), Tito Yepes, Grégoire Garsous, Renaud Foucart, and Caroline Bahnson, all consultants for the World Bank. The study also builds on the outcomes of background papers developed by Robert Bacon, Antonio Estache, Renaud Foucart, and Grégoire Garsous, as well as Hayat Taleb Al-Harazi (Operation Analyst), Josef Loening (Economist), Deepali Tewari (Senior Municipal Development Specialist), Cecilia Maria Paradi-Guilford (ET Consultant), Caroline Van Den Berg (Lead Water and Sanitation Specialist), and Vincent Vesin (Transport Specialist).

The study is a joint effort of the Chief Economist Office and Sustainable Development Unit of the World Bank's Middle East and North Africa (MENA) region and was prepared under the guidance of Caroline Freund (Chief Economist, MENA Region), Laszlo Lovei (Sector Director, MNSSD), and Jonathan Walters (Regional Strategy and Programs Director, MNARS). The study also benefited from the comments and guidance of the three peer reviewers: Moustafa Baher El-Hifnawy (Lead Transport Specialist), Jordan Schwartz (Lead Economist), and Rebekka Grun (Senior Economist).

About the Authors

Antonio Estache is professor of economics at Université Libre de Bruxelles in Belgium and a research fellow at the European Center for Advanced Research in Economics and Statistics (ECARES), Brussels, and the Center for Economic Policy Research (CEPR) in London. He has also served as chief economist of the World Bank's Sustainable Development Vice Presidency and as senior economic advisor for the Poverty Reduction and Economic Management Vice Presidency.

Elena Ianchovichina is lead economist at the Chief Economist Office of the World Bank's Middle East and North Africa region. Prior to this, she managed the program on inclusive growth in the Economic Policy and Debt Department of the World Bank. She has also served in the World Bank's Research Department and East Asia and Pacific region.

Robert Bacon is a consultant at the World Bank Group and an expert on infrastructure and energy issues. He has extensive experience on these issues in different country contexts.

Ilhem Salamon is a senior energy economist in the Energy Sector Group of the World Bank's Middle East and North Africa region. She also has experience working on sustainable development issues in Africa.

Abbreviations

CIM	Construction, installation, and manufacture
FTE	Full-time equivalents
GCC	Gulf Cooperation Council
GDP	Gross domestic product
ICT	Information and communication technology
ILO	International Labour Organization
IMF	International Monetary Fund
IO	Input-output
ISIC	International standard industrial classification
LAC	Latin America and Caribbean
LE	Egyptian Pound
MDG	Millennium Development Goal
MENA	Middle East and North Africa
O&M	Operations and maintenance
OEC	Developing oil exporting country
OIC	Oil importing country
TEU	Twenty-foot equivalent units (containers)
WDI	World Development Indicators

Overview

General Context

Lack of job opportunities, especially for young people, is a well-known, major issue in the Middle East and North Africa (MENA). The region's labor force has been growing at a rapid pace—a consequence of relatively high population growth over the years and rising female labor force participation, but job creation has been lagging. This study assesses the potential for job creation through infrastructure investment in the MENA region. The need to achieve tangible employment results relatively quickly has become urgent in the context of the Arab Spring events. Moreover, heightened regional and global uncertainty has temporarily restrained private investment—the traditional source of new jobs in expanding economies.

Effectively directed and fostered, infrastructure investment has a deep and far-reaching impact on economic development. Infrastructure projects can serve as a potential source of immediate jobs and can boost long-term growth and employment. They can also help meet social goals. Improved provision of high-quality basic infrastructure services, such as hospitals, schools, and water supply and sanitation, raises living standards and improves employability of populations and prospects for inclusive growth.

MENA countries already have experience in making huge infrastructure investments. The region has indeed been investing in infrastructure over the years. Both in the 1990s and 2000s, public investment spending in MENA was higher than in most developing regions, largely because of robust spending in the oil exporting countries, which benefited from rising fuel prices. Spending on infrastructure boosted employment in the construction sector, which was a major source of job growth in the 2000s relative to other sectors and countries. The study shows that maintaining and spreading the momentum in infrastructure investment will be important to support growth and job creation. To do so, policy makers will have to recognize that there are large differences in the initial conditions across the region in terms of starting stocks, needs, fiscal commitments, and potential for job creation.

Variations in the Status of Infrastructure Development

Although infrastructure investment in the region overall has been strong, there is wide variation across countries in the quality and quantity of infrastructure. The high-income Gulf Cooperation Council (GCC) group has the best infrastructure endowments and services in the region, reflecting advanced stage of development and commitment to infrastructure investments financed by oil revenues. However, infrastructure deficiencies in developing MENA remain a concern. Public investment spending has been particularly weak in the oil importing countries (OICs), which have much more limited fiscal space than the oil exporting countries.

While public investment rates increased in the oil exporting countries in the 2000s relative to the 1990s, the opposite happened in the OICs. Recent growth in public-private partnerships was beginning to close the gap in some OICs, but the economic consequences of the Arab uprisings, combined with economic difficulties in Europe, have strained fiscal budgets in developing MENA and reduced private investment, with possible negative consequences for infrastructure spending.

The complexity of identifying infrastructure needs stems not only from differences in the quality and quantity of infrastructure endowments and services across countries but also from differences in needs within countries and sectors. Moreover, under a business as usual scenario, the gaps are likely to magnify as demand for infrastructure grows with population and income growth, and countries face challenges related to water and energy conservation, efficiency, and climate change.

Variations in Infrastructure Needs

The overall needs are quite large. This study estimates MENA's infrastructure investment and maintenance needs through 2020 at about US$106 billion per year or 6.9 percent of the annual regional gross domestic product (GDP). The estimated differences in needs across subregions are just as impressive. Developing oil exporting countries (OECs) are expected to commit almost 11 percent of their GDP annually (US$48 billion) on improving and maintaining their national infrastructure endowments, whereas the OICs and the GCC oil exporters will need approximately 6 and 5 percent of their GDP, respectively, to ensure enough infrastructure to meet their growth and poverty reduction targets (figure O.1).

Investment and rehabilitation needs are likely to be especially high in the electricity and transport sectors, particularly roads. Electricity and transport are each estimated to account for about 43 percent of total infrastructure needs in MENA, followed by information and communication technology (9 percent) and water and sanitation (5 percent). Fulfilling the electricity need alone would require approximately 3 percent of the annual regional GDP, or US$46 billion, of which US$10 billion will be spent in OICs and around US$36 billion in OECs. During the next decade, developing OICs in MENA will need to spend about US$86 billion on upgrading their transport networks, whereas the developing and GCC oil exporters will need US$225 billion and US$145 billion, respectively. Rehabilitation needs are expected to account for slightly more than half of the total infrastructure needs.

Figure O.1   Infrastructure Needs and Financing

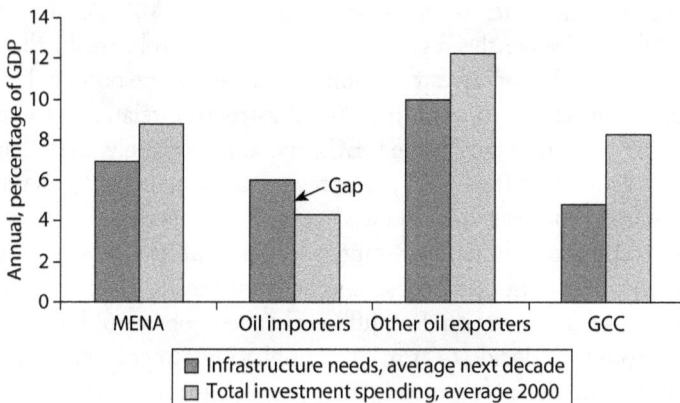

Sources: World Bank and World Bank Private Participation Infrastructure Database.
Note: GCC = Gulf Cooperation Council; GDP = gross domestic product; MENA = Middle East and North Africa.

Variations in Commitments to Meet the Infrastructure Needs

While oil exporters will be able to meet their national infrastructure needs if they maintain investment spending at rates prevailing in the 2000s, oil importers will fall short. Since the vast majority of funding for infrastructure comes from public budgets, it will be critical to protect public investment budgets and try to increase resources going to the sector in the case of oil importers. Doing so will be a smart choice for governments looking to create jobs and growth. The fiscal challenge will be the toughest for the poorest countries of the region since they are the least likely to be able to attract private financing for infrastructure needed to meet the needs of populations.

Variations in Infrastructure's Employment Potential

MENA's infrastructure sectors, including construction and infrastructure services, employ close to one-fifth of the regional workforce or 18.2 million people; of these, 10.7 million workers are employed in the construction sector, whereas the remaining 7.5 million provide infrastructure services. Within infrastructure services, the transport and communication sectors are the biggest employers, representing jointly about 7 percent of the total employment, with energy and water sectors accounting for approximately 1 percent. These aggregate numbers hide significant variations across countries, as the Islamic Republic of Iran, for example, employs more than 40 percent of the country's workforce in the construction and infrastructure sectors, whereas the Arab Republic of Egypt and the Republic of Yemen employ just around 10 percent.

In addition to being a large employer, the infrastructure sector has the potential to contribute to employment creation in MENA, although it alone will not resolve the region's unemployment problem. In the short run, every US$1 billion invested in infrastructure has the potential of generating, on average, around 110,000 infrastructure-related jobs in the OICs, close to 49,000 jobs in the OECs, and approximately 26,000 jobs in the GCC economies (table O.1). The region could therefore generate 2.5 million direct, indirect, and induced infrastructure-related jobs just by meeting estimated annual investment needs, but the potential varies greatly across countries, and these jobs account for less than 2 percent of the labor force in the region. Put differently, these jobs would never materialize if countries decide to trim their public investment rates going forward. Infrastructure investments could provide a quick response and be part of the solution to the unemployment challenge, but infrastructure alone will not resolve this problem.

Table O.1   Infrastructure-Related Short-Term Job Creation

	Infrastructure needs (US$billions)	Direct jobs/ US$billion	Total jobs[a]/ US$billion	Labor force (thousands) in 2009	Direct jobs as a share of the labor force (percent)	Total jobs as a share of the labor force (percent)
GCC	15.8	20,859	26,194	16,387	2.01	2.53
OIC	10.3	86,566	109,236	61,598	1.45	1.83
OEC	20.7	39,454	48,573	52,884	1.54	1.90
Total	46.8	2,037,900[b]	2,544,457[b]	130,869	1.56	1.94

Source: World Bank data.
Note: GCC = Gulf Cooperation Council; OEC = developing oil exporting country; OIC = oil importing country.
a. Total jobs include direct, indirect, and induced jobs created per US$1 billion in the short run.
b. The estimate of total direct jobs in the last row of the table refers to the jobs created by meeting annual infrastructure needs. This estimate is obtained by multiplying the estimated infrastructure needs for a particular group with the corresponding direct jobs estimated per US$1 billion, and then summing up across groups.

Figure O.2   Cost of a Direct Job in Roads and Bridge Construction Relative to Other Sectors in 2009

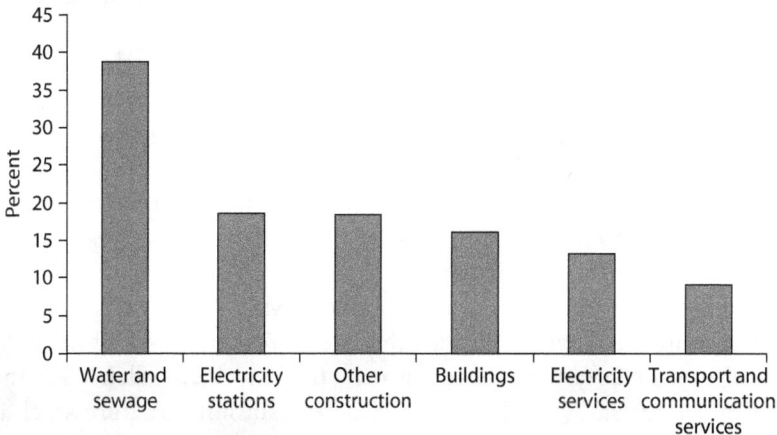

Source: World Bank data.

Because of per capita income differences, spending of US$1 billion generates more than six times as many jobs in a sector in low-income Djibouti than in upper middle-income Lebanon, but the latter would find it easier to finance investment expenditure. Spending on construction of roads and bridges would generate more jobs as the same amount of spending in any other infrastructure sector. This is because the cost of an infrastructure job in the roads and bridge construction sector is less than one-fifth of the cost of a job in the electricity-generating sector, and slightly less than one-tenth of the cost of a job in the transport and communication services sector (figure O.2).

Sectors also differ in their propensity to generate indirect jobs. It depends on the extent to which the sector requires inputs from other sectors to produce its output. In Egypt, the ratio of all jobs to the number of direct jobs was as low as 1.09 for construction in roads and bridges, whereas it was 1.82 for transport and communication. This indicates that when investment decisions are made with the objective of creating jobs, consideration should be given to both direct and indirect employment effects, as well as the type of skills required to implement projects.

The long-term employment effect of infrastructure investment could be significant. The study finds that the employment response induced by infrastructure investment resulting in 1 percentage point additional growth is expected to be 9 million additional jobs in the course of 10 years in MENA or a little less than 1 million jobs per year. Such a response is significant as it accounts for approximately 30 percent of the jobs created in the region during the 2000s. Had these jobs been created during the last decade, the unemployment rate would be substantially lower than the 10 percent registered in 2009.

The infrastructure investment required to boost growth by a percentage point would vary by country. The lower the growth elasticity with respect to infrastructure, the higher the required increase in the stock of infrastructure. For example, the lower bound of the elasticity suggests that an increase of 8.7 percent in the stock of infrastructure is required to add a percentage point to growth in the MENA region. This is the more likely scenario in high-income MENA, comprising the GCC economies and some upper middle-income MENA countries, whereas in the more developed countries the likely growth impact of an additional unit of infrastructure investment tends to be smaller. With the upper bound elasticity, the required increase in infrastructure stock is just 3.1 percent.

A switch to labor-intensive technology could enhance the employment creation effect of infrastructure investment, and it may also reduce overall costs. The study discusses the possibility of doing so in the maintenance of unpaved roads and finds that the use of labor-intensive technology reduces investment needs in the region by 0.3 percent of GDP. But, solely focusing on costs is probably not the best criterion when considering labor-intensive technologies. The cost structure of labor-intensive infrastructure provision is different from equipment-intensive alternatives, as it includes components like training or development of institutional capacity. Direct comparisons of labor versus nonlabor costs can therefore be misleading.

Policy Implications

Infrastructure investment has the potential to create jobs quickly, while providing a foundation for future growth. This is especially important in the OICs, where the infrastructure gap is the greatest and employment needs are growing. However, it is also likely to be most difficult in these countries because of strained finances. Going forward, government decisions on what types of spending to expand and what to downsize in order to achieve balanced budgets will have important implications for jobs. In designing country-specific solutions, governments will have to take on predictable challenges: the governance of job creation, the proper targeting and fiscal cost assessment of subsidies needed to create jobs, the design and fiscal costs of the (re)training programs needed, and the expectations on the job creation effects of infrastructure.

Governance Challenge

Prudent infrastructure development will be critical for short- and long-term growth and job creation because the greatest risk to using infrastructure as part of an employment and growth strategy in MENA countries is poor governance. Not all jobs are equal in terms of skills, and not all infrastructure investments are equal in terms of ability to create jobs for different skills. This means that investments in infrastructure will need to be prioritized based on the employment and infrastructure needs and opportunities in the country. For example, road and bridge construction projects will have a direct impact on creation of relatively low-skilled jobs. These types of projects will be especially effective in addressing job-related concerns in countries where there is a large pool of relatively unskilled and unemployed nationals. This is the case in most MENA countries, where the majority of the unemployed do not have tertiary education (figure O.3). By contrast, projects in transport and communication services have large indirect effects and, therefore, the ability to create a diverse set of jobs for workers with different skill levels. These projects will appeal to policy makers in countries where the unemployed have the ability to acquire specialized skills relatively quickly.

Subsidy Targeting Challenge

Public works and different types of subsidized employment programs have been used widely to make it easier for people who cannot find unsubsidized jobs to find employment and acquire on-the-job skills. These programs are necessary, for instance, to address structural issues,

Figure O.3   Shares of Unemployed by Education Level in Selected MENA Economies

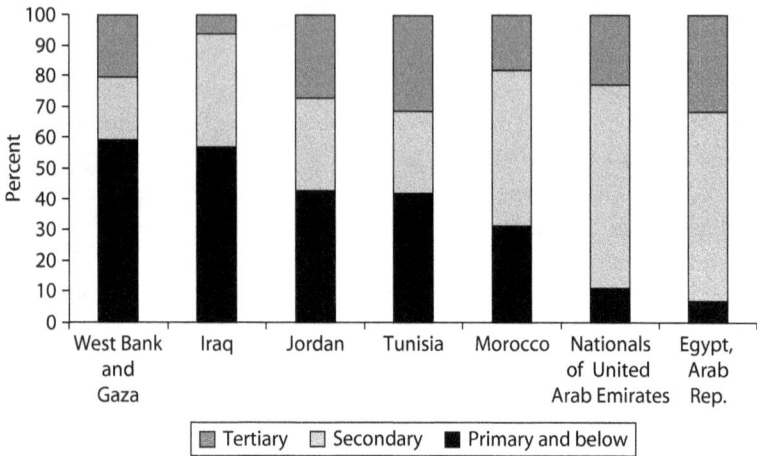

Source: World Bank data.
Note: MENA = Middle East and North Africa.

which will not be addressed through market forces alone as economies grow bigger. Subsidies to job creation in infrastructure and construction will have to be designed to make the most of employment opportunities for low-skilled workers. The design of the targeting will also have to address the pressing nature of the need to create jobs. Indeed, boosting short-term job creation in MENA is desirable, particularly in the context of the recent political developments. But subsidized employment programs are costly and should be designed to ensure that there is a positive spillover to long-run employment and employability.

Employment Subsidies Costing and Financing Challenge

The net costs of subsidizing job creation are difficult to estimate, although the temporary nature of the subsidies, which last only during the investment phase of an infrastructure project, minimizes any potential losses. In addition to the direct fiscal costs of providing the subsidies and any associated training and program management, there are less obvious costs in the form of deadweight loss, substitution, and displacement effects. The costs would also be overestimated if the induced formalization of the labor market and hence the potential revenue from labor taxes are ignored, and underestimated if this formalization leads quickly to added expenses in unemployment benefits and other indirect related costs. There is also the opportunity cost of how the funds are spent. In an economy with poor institutional quality and high levels of rent-seeking behavior, public spending on infrastructure could lead to projects with low value added and cost overruns. Thus, good governance is a key complement to infrastructure spending.

Training Challenge

Experience shows that the long-term payoffs of employment subsidies can be achieved only if subsidized employment programs are combined with training and counseling. Therefore, the design of these programs should be given as much attention as the design of the subsidized employment programs. Specific training should be considered only if there is market demand for these qualifications or if there is a need to buy time in a labor market restructuring transition. Often, general training supporting labor market flexibility will be sufficient and more efficient in increasing productivity than specialized training.

Challenge of Managing Expectations

The study shows that infrastructure investments could provide a relatively quick, short-term response to MENA's unemployment challenge. As such, it is part of the solution, but infrastructure alone will not resolve the problem. Infrastructure and construction jobs represent less than 20 percent of the jobs in most countries of the region. Even a dramatic increase in labor-intensive infrastructure investments and maintenance would not be able to address the very large unemployment rate of the region. Countries should press on with reforms that improve the business environment, especially business regulations and governance. The importance of a sound regulatory environment and good governance for inclusive growth has been underscored in numerous studies. This study focused on estimating the employment impact of infrastructure investment in MENA. In the future, more work needs to be done to assess the impact of infrastructure investment on different types of labor, for example, skilled versus unskilled, young versus old, and domestic versus migrant workers.

CHAPTER 1

Introduction

The state of national labor markets has always been a concern for governments and development agencies such as the World Bank. Key labor market indicators, such as the rate of unemployment, send signals about the health of an economy and mirror citizens' attitudes. Being gainfully employed is an important aspect of an individual's well-being both financially and socially, as "initial failures in finding a job can lead to persistent joblessness, a loss of interest in further schooling, delayed family formation, mental distress, and negative manifestations of citizenship" (World Bank 2007). Importantly, high unemployment tends to increase the risk of violence, and unemployment and idleness are the most cited reasons for young people to join gangs and rebel groups (World Bank 2011a).

The Arab Spring events of 2011 brought to the fore concerns about high unemployment, especially among the youth in the countries of the Middle East and North Africa (MENA). This region is facing daunting employment challenges. The unemployment rate in MENA has been higher than in any other region in the world, and has been especially high among youth (World Bank 2004). At the same time, the labor force has been growing at a rapid pace—the consequence of relatively high population growth over the years and also increasing female labor force participation.

Reforms intended at improving the competitiveness and the investment climate of MENA economies and strengthening the employability of workers are key factors in boosting job creation, especially for young people in MENA. However, the effects of such reforms would only be felt gradually, whereas the urgency of the employment challenge in the context of the Arab Spring events calls for policies that have an immediate impact on job creation. These will be particularly helpful, given the heightened regional and global uncertainty, which has temporarily restrained private investment—the traditional source of new jobs in expanding economies. This report therefore focuses on investment in infrastructure, which has the potential to create jobs quickly, while providing a foundation for future growth.

It is well known that, if effectively directed and fostered, infrastructure investments will have deep and far-reaching impacts on economic and social development. Infrastructure investments have the potential to immediately boost employment by creating jobs in construction and infrastructure services. These investments in turn boost employment in sectors that either supply inputs to infrastructure projects directly or indirectly, or supply goods and services to meet the extra demand created by the additional income of those benefiting directly and indirectly from the infrastructure spending. The infrastructure built by these investments in turn increases the need for sustainable employment in operation and maintenance and creates a foundation for growth of enterprises, enabling them to expand operations and employment. The social payoff of developing sustainable and integrated basic infrastructure is also significant. Improved provision of high-quality basic infrastructure services, such as hospitals, schools, and water supply and sanitation, raises living standards and increases employability of populations and prospects for inclusive growth.

Increased expenditure on infrastructure projects has a short-run effect on employment creation as more workers are hired to build infrastructure. These jobs last only during the investment phase of the project, and, without a continuous injection as in a stimulus-type program, such jobs will be temporary. However, the investment program will have created a larger stock of infrastructure capital and this permanent addition facilitates additional growth in the economy. The extra demand from this incremental growth creates more jobs, and these tend to be permanent. Furthermore, an employment experience in an infrastructure-related employment program, even if temporary, might improve the chance of being re-employed at a later date. This study capitalizes on the World Bank's long-standing knowledge on infrastructure, employment, and growth and applies it to the case of MENA to assess the employment creation potential of infrastructure investment.

Background Information

MENA countries have been investing in infrastructure over the years. Both in the 1990s and 2000s, public investment spending in MENA was higher than in most developing regions, largely because of robust spending in the oil exporting countries, which benefited from rising fuel prices (figure 1.1). Spending on infrastructure boosted employment in the

Figure 1.1   Public Gross Fixed Capital Formation
averages, percentage of GDP

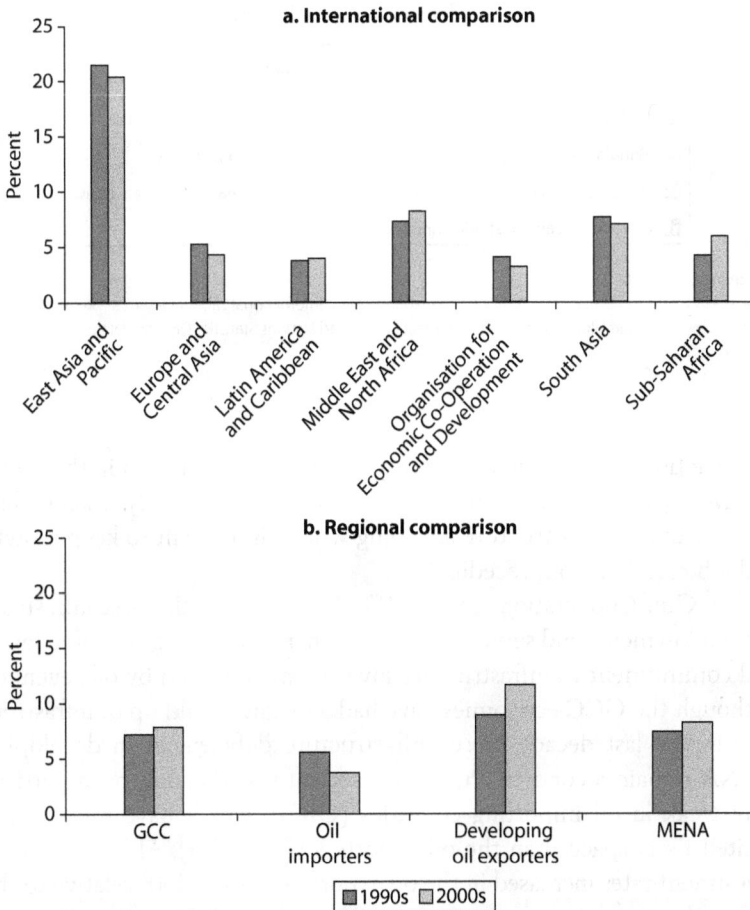

a. International comparison

b. Regional comparison

1990s   2000s

Source: World Bank 2011b.
Note: GCC = Gulf Cooperation Council; MENA = Middle East and North Africa. Numbers are weighted averages of data from the International Monetary Fund/International Financial Statistics (IMF/IFS) for a balanced sample of countries in each region.

Figure 1.2   Sectors' Contribution to Annual Employment Growth in the 2000s

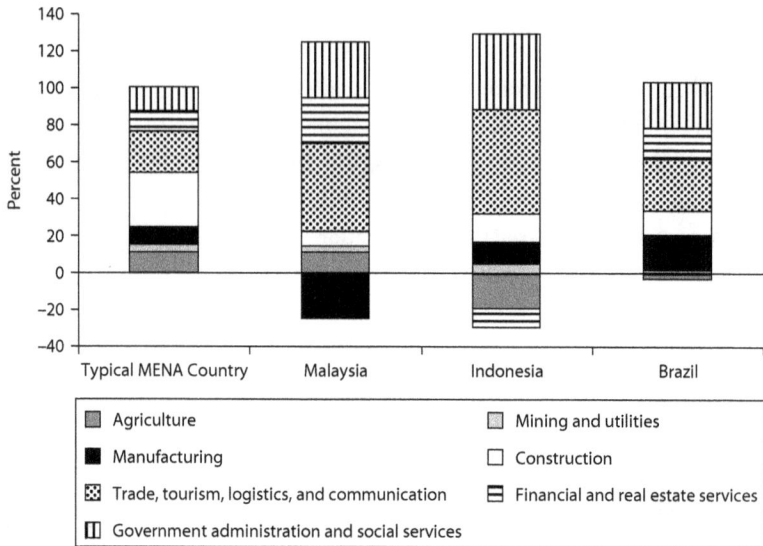

Source: World Bank 2011b.
Note: MENA = Middle East and North Africa. Calculations rely on International Labour Organization data for employment by sector and Global Trade Analysis Project and United Nations Statistics Division data on value added by sector.

construction sector, which was a major source of job growth in the 2000s relative to other sectors and other countries (figure 1.2). Maintaining momentum in infrastructure spending will be important to keep growth and job creation from receding.

The Gulf Cooperation Council (GCC) group has the best infrastructure endowments and services in the region, reflecting high-income levels and commitment to infrastructure investments financed by oil revenues. Although the GCC economies have had a massive build up of infrastructure in the last decade or so, infrastructure deficiencies in developing MENA remain a concern. Public investment spending has been particularly weak in oil importing countries (OICs), which have much more limited fiscal space than the oil exporters (figure 1.3). Although public investment rates increased in the oil exporters in the 2000s relative to the 1990s, the opposite happened in the OICs (figure 1.1).

Recent growth in public-private partnerships was beginning to fill the gap in some OICs. However, the economic consequences of the Arab uprisings, combined with economic difficulties in Europe, have strained

Figure 1.3   Fiscal Space Indicators

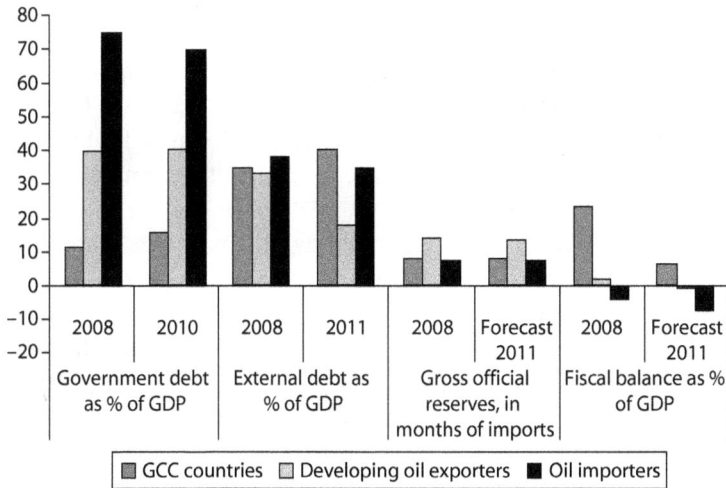

Sources: World Bank data, IMF, and government sources.
Note: FY = fiscal year; GCC = Gulf Cooperation Council; GDP = gross domestic product.

fiscal budgets in developing MENA and reduced private investment, with possible negative consequences for infrastructure spending. Thus, going forward, it will be critical to protect public investment budgets and increase resources for infrastructure projects in the case of oil importers. Doing so will be a smart choice for governments looking to create jobs and growth.

Scope and Structure of the Study

This study consists of five chapters. Following the introductory chapter is chapter 2, which provides an overview of the current labor market structure in MENA as well as a summary of the future challenges the region faces in providing employment options for its citizens. It then gives an overview of the status of MENA's infrastructure endowments and calculates the domestic needs for infrastructure over the coming decade. Based on the current share of labor used in the infrastructure sector, the chapter finally assesses the general potential for the sector to assist in job creation in the region.

Chapter 3 assesses the short-run impact of infrastructure investments on job creation—direct, indirect, and induced. The chapter examines various ways of doing this, drawing on project information as well as adapting and using available input-output tables. For this purpose, the chapter takes advantage of a comprehensive study on infrastructure-employment linkages in Latin America and the Caribbean and adapts its findings to the MENA region.

Chapter 4 examines the long-term impact of infrastructure investments on economic growth and employment generation. It employs infrastructure- and employment-growth elasticities in order to estimate the potential benefits of infrastructure investments for employment creation between 2010 and 2020.

Chapter 5 discusses the issues faced by policy makers when considering the use of subsidized employment schemes as part of infrastructure investment programs. The chapter discusses in particular how such short-term employment programs can be used to improve the long-term employment prospects of workers through suitable training and education. The chapter addresses both questions of incentives and efficiency.

Definitions and Key Concepts

The MENA region is heterogeneous, so in addition to reporting regional aggregates, this study reports statistics on three commonly used country groupings—the members of the GCC countries, OECs, and OICs. Table 1.1 shows the distribution of the economies in MENA according to this classification, along with their income categories: high-income (H), higher middle-income (HM), lower middle-income (LM), and low-income (L). Developing MENA refers to the OICs and OECs.

For detailed analysis of job creation, it is important to distinguish between the jobs created within the sector where the initial investment takes place, and those jobs created outside the sector but linked to the

Table 1.1   MENA Classification

Developing oil importers		Developing oil exporters		Gulf Cooperation Council	
Economy	Income bracket	Economy	Income bracket	Economy	Income bracket
Djibouti	L	Algeria	HM	Bahrain	H
Egypt, Arab Rep.	LM	Iran, Islamic Rep.	HM	Kuwait	H
Jordan	LM	Iraq	LM	Oman	H
Lebanon	HM	Libya	HM	Qatar	H
Morocco	LM	Syrian Arab Republic	LM	Saudi Arabia	H
Tunisia	LM	Yemen, Rep.	L	United Arab Emirates	H
West Bank and Gaza	LM				

Note: H = high-income; HM = higher middle-income; L = low-income; LM = lower middle-income.

original investment. Conventionally, three categories are distinguished when analyzing the employment effects of investment.

Direct employment refers to the employment created within a given sector as it responds to an increase in the final demand for its product such as the employment created to manufacture a wind turbine and then to operate it. The ratio of the number of direct jobs created to the increment in spending is termed the direct employment multiplier.

Indirect employment refers to the employment created as other sectors expand their outputs in order to supply the inputs required to produce the output of the given sector, and the employment created by yet other sectors as they respond to the demand for their outputs from the sectors supplying the given sector. For example, the manufacture of steel to supply turbine components creates indirect employment, as does the extra energy required to produce the steel. The ratio of indirect plus direct jobs to direct jobs is named type I multiplier, and the sum of direct plus indirect jobs is termed type I jobs.

Induced employment refers to the employment created to meet the extra demand created by the additional household income of those benefiting directly and indirectly from the initial increase in final demand for the given sector. The extra workers in the turbine industry, the steel industry, and the power sector spend part of their incomes on a whole range of goods, thus creating extra employment in these sectors, and this creates yet further spending and employment from these incomes. The fraction of extra income spent on goods and services is a crucial parameter, which depends on the tax and savings rates applicable to the workers benefiting directly and indirectly by the initial investment. The ratio of direct plus indirect plus induced jobs to direct jobs is called type II multiplier, and the sum of the three categories is termed type II jobs.

For each of these categories of employment, the time dimension is important. Investment spending generates jobs in construction, installation, and manufacture (CIM) as well as possible jobs in operations and maintenance (O&M). The duration of the CIM jobs depends on the nature of the investment, whereas the duration of O&M jobs is linked to plant life. Furthermore, some jobs will be full time and some part time. Conventionally, jobs are converted to full-time equivalents (FTEs) and expressed in terms of job-years, so as to allow for the possibility that a given investment expenditure will generate jobs stretching over a number of years. This aspect of employment calculation requires careful specification of the way in which the expenditure is to be made.

The calculation of long-term job creation through the links from infrastructure to growth and growth to employment encompasses all three types of employment, as it links total employment to total infrastructure spending.

References

World Bank. 2004. *Unlocking the Employment Potential in the Middle East and North Africa.* Washington, DC: World Bank.

———. 2007. *World Development Report: Development and the Next Generation.* Washington, DC: World Bank. http://www-wds.worldbank.org/external/default/WDSContentServer/WDSP/IB/2006/09/13/000112742_20060913111024/Rendered/PDF/359990WDR0complete.pdf.

———. 2011a. *World Development Report: Conflict, Security and Development.* Washington, DC: World Bank. http://wdr2011.worldbank.org/fulltext.

———. 2011b. *Economic Developments and Prospects Report, Middle East and North Africa: Investing for Growth and Jobs.* Washington, DC: World Bank. http://siteresources.worldbank.org/INTMENA/Resources/World_Bank_MENA_Economic_Developments_Prospects_Sept2011.pdf.

CHAPTER 2

The State of Employment and Infrastructure and Future Needs

This chapter provides an overview of the current employment situation in the Middle East and North Africa (MENA) region, employment in infrastructure, and assessment of the region's infrastructure endowments, as well as future domestic infrastructure needs. These assessments highlight the magnitude of the challenges faced by governments in the region and enable us to provide a rough estimate of the scope of infrastructure investment in solving the region's unemployment problem in the coming decade.

Employment Challenges

The supply and demand of workers and jobs are the underlying factors that define labor market dynamics in an economy. Employment levels indicate the actual demand for workers in a regional economy, whereas the labor force numbers show the potential demand for jobs among the population of the region. Hence, unemployment exists where the labor force exceeds employment. Table 2.1 shows the growth trends in employment and labor force sizes in the MENA region between 2000 and 2009.[1]

Table 2.1   Employment and the Size of the Labor Force in MENA

Region	Employment (thousands)		Labor force (thousands)	
	2000	2009	2000	2009
Gulf Cooperation Council (GCC) countries	10,995	15,473	11,511	16,387
Developing oil exporting countries (OECs)	39,588	54,742	47,187	61,598
Oil importing countries (OICs)	37,168	47,323	41,954	52,884
Total MENA	87,751	117,538	100,653	130,869

Source: International Labour Organization (ILO).
Note: MENA = Middle East and North Africa.

Table 2.1 shows that, in spite of approximately 30 million jobs being created during the past decade, the size of the labor force has concurrently grown by a little more than 30 million leading to an increased gap between labor force supply and available jobs—a gap that is widening at the rate of about 0.33 percent per year. While the number of unemployed increased, labor force participation increased too, so the region-wide unemployment rate declined by 3 percentage points from 13 percent in 2000 to 10 percent in 2009.

Employment creation in the MENA region needs to accelerate during the next decade to bring down unemployment further and accommodate new entrants into the labor force. Less than 3 million jobs were created annually in the 2000s, but the region should have created 1 million more jobs to bring down unemployment rates between 4 and 6 percent—a range prevalent in fast-growing economies. This is a more modest estimate than the one presented in a 2004 World Bank report, which argued that the labor force of the region would increase from 104 million workers in 2000 to 146 million by 2010 and then to 185 million by 2020 (World Bank 2004). The report concluded that, to cope with unemployment and growth in the labor force, almost 100 million new jobs would have to be created over the next two decades, amounting to 5 million jobs a year or 2 million more jobs than the ones created in the 2000s.

The more modest estimate of 1 million additional jobs in the 2000s suggests that the goal of solving the problem of unemployment is within reach. Of course, achieving this regional goal would depend on developments in a few major economies. Labor force levels by country in 2009 (figure 2.1) indicate that the Arab Republic of Egypt and the Islamic Republic of Iran, followed by Algeria and Morocco, have the largest labor forces. Thus, labor market developments in Egypt and the Islamic

Figure 2.1   Labor Force Levels in MENA, 2009

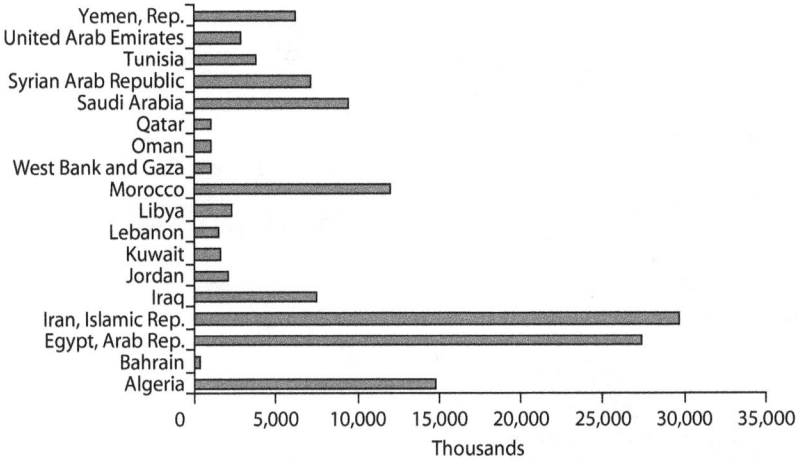

Source: International Labour Organization (ILO).
Note: MENA = Middle East and North Africa.

Republic of Iran have a much greater impact on regional outcomes than other countries in the region.

Infrastructure Endowments and Future Needs

MENA has one of the highest levels of infrastructure endowments among developing regions (table 2.2). The region, taken as a whole, has the best access to electricity, and it has the second best paved road network and water and sanitation systems in the developing world. The region's electricity generating capacity is comparable to that of the East Asia and Pacific region and South Asia.

Although the infrastructure investment in the overall region has been strong, intraregional differences in infrastructure endowments and quality of infrastructure services are substantial and in line with differences in per capita incomes. The Gulf Cooperation Council (GCC) group has the best infrastructure endowment in the region and by far the best provision of paved road network, telephone density, and electricity generating capacity. For example, the density of the paved road network in the GCC group is 27 times greater than that in the developing oil exporting countries (OECs), and five times more than that of the developing oil importing countries (OICs) (table 2.3). When it comes to access to basic services, the gaps among the three groups are much smaller, although it

Table 2.2   Infrastructure Endowments in the Developing World
averages, 2005–08

Sector	EAP	ECA	LAC	MENA	SA	SSA
Density of paved road network						
km per 1,000 km² of arable land	1,128	1,051	2,965	2,179	467	1,095
Telephone density						
Fixed and mobile subscribers per 1,000 people	400	929	839	537	353	273
Electricity generating capacity						
Million kWh per million people	0.30	0.92	0.44	0.30	0.31	0.11
Access to electricity						
% of population with access	62	n.a.	86	91	48	31
Improved water						
% of population with access	81	94	91	88	82	67
Improved sanitation						
% of population with access	62	90	78	83	55	33

Source: World Bank Development Indicators.
Note: EAP = East Asia and Pacific; ECA = Europe and Central Asia; km² = kilometers squared; kWh = kilowatts per hour; LAC = Latin America and the Caribbean; MENA = Middle East and North Africa; n.a. = not applicable; SA = South Asia; SSA = Sub-Saharan Africa.

Table 2.3   Infrastructure Endowments in MENA by Country Grouping
averages, 2005–08

Sector	OIC	OEC	GCC
Density of paved road network			
km per 1,000 km² of arable land	3,220	618	16,907
Telephone density			
Fixed and mobile subscribers per 1,000 people	535	538	1,351
Electricity generating capacity			
Million kWh per million people	0.3	0.4	2.9
Access to electricity			
% of population with access	98	85	98
Improved water			
% of population with access	93	79	97
Improved sanitation			
% of population with access	84	81	99

Source: World Bank Development Indicators.
Note: GCC = Gulf Cooperation Council; km² = kilometers squared; kWh = kilowatts per hour; MENA = Middle East and North Africa; OEC = developing oil exporting country; OIC = oil importing country.

is worth noting that basic services have slightly higher penetration rates in OICs compared with OECs.

Income and population growth, and baseline endowments are key determinants of the demand for infrastructure services and investment needs, going forward. Investment in infrastructure should, at least, maintain infrastructure services to satisfy the demand of consumers and producers, including the expansion of access to basic services, because of population growth. This section presents estimates of the investment needs in infrastructure for the decade starting after 2010 by considering determinants of demand for infrastructure services for the three main groups of countries in MENA.

The assessment of future infrastructure needs is based on econometric models of demand for each infrastructure subsector following Fay and Yepes (2003) and Ianchovichina et al. (2012). The models are estimated on a worldwide dataset, although with a partial coverage of regions, including MENA (see annex 2A for econometric results and annex 2B for data sources). The database used for these estimations is an annual panel data of infrastructure stocks, macroeconomic variables, and demographic characteristics. Data for MENA countries cover years up to 2008. The data are taken mainly from the World Bank's World Development Indicators (WDI) complemented with material from country official statistical offices and other multilateral organizations.[2] The annual gross domestic product (GDP) growth rate for the world as a whole is assumed to be 3.5 percent per year in the period 2011–20, whereas that for MENA is 4.3 percent. OICs are assumed to grow at 3.5 percent per year, whereas OECs and GCC economies are assumed to grow at 4.6 percent and 4.5 percent, respectively.[3] Demographic trends are taken from the 2009 United Nations World Urbanization Prospects.

This assessment improves upon earlier ones conducted for the MENA region by (1) including data on infrastructure stocks for countries of the region from national sources as compared to relying on extrapolations from international databases, (2) updating the data from original international sources, and (3) including high-income GCC economies in the definition of MENA.

The infrastructure needs are estimated based on the levels of infrastructure endowments required to meet household and firm demands. The approach relies on an econometric estimate of this future demand for infrastructure. Future demands depend on technology, the real price of infrastructure services, per capita income, and the share of GDP derived from agriculture and manufacturing sectors.[4] Projected levels of infrastructure stocks are valued at the unit costs used in Ianchovichina et al. (2012) and shown in table 2.4.

To assess the full budgetary allocation needed by the various sectors, estimates of the associated maintenance needs are included as well. Maintenance is needed for any investment to meet its assumed lifetime, so a commitment to maintenance is built into the cost-benefit

Table 2.4   Unit Costs of Infrastructure by Sector
U.S. dollars

Sector	Cost per unit	Unit	Depreciation rate (%)
Electricity generation	2,000	kW	4.0
Paved roads	410,000	km	4.7
Unpaved roads	50,000	km	7.2
Rail lines	900,000	km	4.0
Rural water and sanitation	150	person	3.0
Urban sanitation	150	person	3.0
Rural sanitation	130	person	3.0
Urban water	80	person	3.0
Main telephone lines[a]	127–580	line	8.0
Mobile lines[a]	127–451	line	8.0
Access to electricity	195	person	4.0
Ports	348	TEU	4.0
Wastewater treatment	120	person	3.0

Source: Ianchovichina et al. 2012.
Note: km = kilometers; kW = kilowatt.
a. Varies by region.

analysis and the calculation of the social rate of return on the investments. In this study, maintenance costs are estimated by multiplying
the stock value in the previous period by a depreciation rate. A fixed
annual depreciation rate is assumed for each sector and shown in table
2.4. For paved and unpaved roads, the depreciation rate comes from a
stylized model of a maintenance and rehabilitation program.[5] It
assumes roads of good quality undergo routine maintenance every year
except for year 5 and 15 when periodic maintenance and rehabilitation takes place, respectively. Consequently, every year, 85 percent of
a country's road network in good or fair condition would be subjected
to routine maintenance, 12 percent would undergo periodic maintenance, and the last 3 percent would be rehabilitated. The model
assumes that roads in bad condition undergo a special rehabilitation
program to reduce their percentage to zero over a 10-year span.[6]
However, not all roads in bad condition will automatically be
improved; some will remain in bad condition while the program
improves the network as a whole. The annual average maintenance
and rehabilitation costs for the period between 2011 and 2020 are
then divided by the unit cost of full replacement to obtain the depreciation rate as shown in table 2.5. This way, the life of the asset and
the cost of keeping its service level are incorporated into the depreciation rate. Estimates of total annual expenditure needs by sector,

Table 2.5   Roads Maintenance and Rehabilitation Program
U.S. dollars

	Capital intensive technology	
Component	Paved roads	Unpaved roads
Unit costs		
Routine	4,000	2,000
Periodic	50,000	10,000
Rehabilitation	150,000	15,000
Maintenance and rehabilitation (annual cost per km)	19,100	3,600
Unit costs for new roads	410,000	50,000
Depreciation rate (%)	4.7	7.2

Source: World Bank data.
Note: km = kilometers.

subgroup, and region are presented in table 2.6. In the absence of data for a sector or subsector in a country, regional averages of investment were imputed to obtain total investment needs (see annex 2C).

Annual additional infrastructure investment and maintenance needs through 2020 for the MENA region are estimated to be US$106 billion or 6.9 percent of the regional GDP. OECs have the highest demand, representing 46 percent of the regional needs, and they will need to commit almost 11 percent of their GDP annually (US$48 billion) to keep up with their economic and demographic growth. The needs of OICs and the GCC economies are smaller at approximately 6 and 5 percent, respectively, of their GDP.

Investment and rehabilitation needs are particularly high in the transport and electricity sectors. These account for 44 and 45 percent of total needs, respectively, followed by information and communication technology (ICT), and water and sanitation. During the next 10 years, OECs will need to spend 5.1 percent of their GDP (or US$22.5 billion) annually on upgrading and expanding their transport networks, whereas OICs and GCC will need to spend around 2.0 percent of their respective GDP.

Approximately 40 percent of infrastructure expenditure meets capital expansion needs, whereas the remainder is allocated to infrastructure maintenance projects (figure 2.2). Of the US$46 billion that should be spent annually in the transport sector to keep up with total demand (table 2.6), about US$30 billion must be earmarked for maintenance as suggested by the expenditure shares required for new capital and for maintenance, as reported in table 2.7.

The vast share of infrastructure expenditure is expected to fund projects that meet the needs for transport and electricity infrastructure. Within

Table 2.6   Annual Expenditure Needs for Infrastructure in the MENA Region

Sector	OIC	OEC	GCC	Total
	Percentage of GDP			
Transport	2.2	5.1	2.0	3.0
Paved roads	1.4	2.7	0.6	1.4
Unpaved roads	0.6	2.1	1.3	1.4
Rail lines	0.1	0.1	0.0	0.1
Ports	0.1	0.1	0.1	0.1
ICT	0.8	1.1	0.2	0.6
Telephone mainlines	0.2	0.3	0.0	0.2
Mobile lines	0.6	0.7	0.2	0.4
Electricity	2.5	4.2	2.5	3.0
Electricity generation	2.1	3.7	2.4	2.7
Electricity access	0.4	0.5	0.1	0.3
Water and sanitation	0.5	0.6	0.1	0.3
Water	0.2	0.2	0.0	0.13
Sanitation	0.3	0.3	0.1	0.19
Total	6.0	10.9	4.8	6.9
	Amount, 2005 US$, million			
Transport	8,575	22,492	14,453	45,519
Paved roads	5,448	12,088	3,956	21,492
Unpaved roads	2,246	9,497	9,461	21,204
Rail lines	428	639	75	1,143
Ports	452	268	960	1,680
ICT	3,021	4,707	1,559	9,287
Telephone mainlines	696	1,464	259	2,419
Mobile lines	2,325	3,243	1,300	6,868
Electricity	9,894	18,607	17,602	46,103
Electricity generation	8,214	16,467	17,139	41,820
Electricity access	1,680	2,140	463	4,283
Water and sanitation	1,764	2,497	647	4,908
Water	745	1,040	190	1,975
Sanitation	1,019	1,458	457	2,934
Total	23,254	48,303	34,261	105,818
Share by country group	22%	46%	32%	100%
Investment	10,261	20,739	15,786	46,786
Maintenance	12,992	27,564	18,475	59,032

Source: World Bank data.
Note: GCC = Gulf Cooperation Council; GDP = gross domestic product; ICT = information and communication technology; MENA = Middle East and North Africa; OEC = developing oil exporting country; OIC = oil importing country.

transport, paved roads are expected to absorb most of the funds and account for more than half of the total transport infrastructure needs in OECs (50 percent), almost two-thirds of the needs in OICs (63 percent), and less than one-third of the needs in GCC countries (28 percent).

Figure 2.2   Composition of Infrastructure Expenditure Needs by Group of Countries

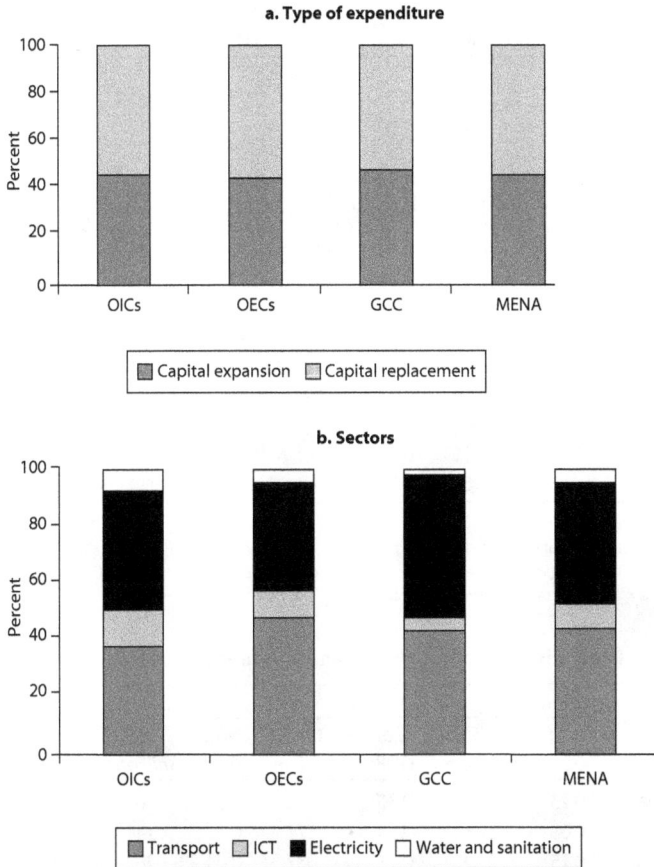

a. Type of expenditure

Legend: Capital expansion / Capital replacement

b. Sectors

Legend: Transport / ICT / Electricity / Water and sanitation

Source: World Bank data.
Note: GCC = Gulf Cooperation Council; ICT = information and communication technology; MENA = Middle East and North Africa; OEC = developing oil exporting country; OIC = oil importing country.

Electricity is the sector with the largest total expenditure needs. Annual needs for electricity amount to US$46 billion per year in MENA, or 3 percent of the regional annual GDP (table 2.6). Ensuring adequate electrification access for 2011–20 is estimated to require US$4 billion per year, whereas the bulk of the annual expenditure (US$42 billion) will be needed to secure adequate levels of generation capacity.

Expenditure needs for ICT will amount to around $9 billion per year between 2011 and 2020 and reflect mostly expenditure on mobile communication infrastructure (table 2.6). The bulk of this expenditure

Table 2.7   Annual Infrastructure Investment and Maintenance Needs in MENA by Type of Investment as Percent of GDP

Sector	OIC N	OIC M	OEC N	OEC M	GCC N	GCC M	Total N	Total M
Transport	0.8	1.4	1.8	3.3	0.7	1.4	1.0	1.9
Paved roads	0.6	0.8	1.1	1.6	0.3	0.3	0.6	0.8
Unpaved roads	0.2	0.4	0.6	1.5	0.4	1.0	0.4	1.0
Rail lines	0.0	0.1	0.0	0.1	0.0	0.0	0.0	0.1
Ports	0.1	0.0	0.0	0.0	0.1	0.1	0.1	0.0
ICT	0.26	0.51	0.42	0.65	0.06	0.16	0.21	0.39
Telephone mainlines	0.08	0.10	0.15	0.18	0.02	0.02	0.07	0.09
Mobile lines	0.18	0.41	0.27	0.47	0.04	0.14	0.14	0.30
Electricity	1.37	1.16	2.22	1.98	1.44	1.04	1.65	1.34
Electricity generation	1.22	0.88	2.04	1.67	1.42	1.00	1.55	1.16
Electricity access	0.15	0.28	0.17	0.31	0.02	0.04	0.10	0.18
Water and sanitation	0.19	0.27	0.28	0.29	0.04	0.05	0.14	0.17
Water	0.07	0.12	0.12	0.12	0.01	0.02	0.06	0.07
Sanitation	0.11	0.15	0.16	0.17	0.03	0.04	0.09	0.10
Total	2.63	3.33	4.68	6.22	2.23	2.61	3.03	3.83

Source: World Bank data
Note: GCC = Gulf Cooperation Council; GDP = gross domestic product; ICT = information and communication technology; M = maintenance; MENA = Middle East and North Africa; N = new capital; OIC = Oil importing country; OEC = Developing oil exporting country.

Table 2.8   Expenditure Needs for Water and Sanitation in Urban and Rural Areas

Subsector	OIC % of GDP	OIC US$, millions	OEC % of GDP	OEC US$, millions	GCC % of GDP	GCC US$, millions	Total % of GDP	Total US$, millions
Urban areas	0.23	888	0.36	1,613	0.06	403	0.19	2,904
Water	0.08	308	0.13	577	0.02	141	0.07	1,025
Sanitation	0.15	580	0.23	1,037	0.04	262	0.12	1,879
Rural areas	0.22	876	0.20	884	0.03	244	0.13	2,004
Water	0.11	437	0.10	463	0.01	49	0.06	949
Sanitation	0.11	439	0.09	421	0.03	195	0.07	1,055

Source: World Bank data.
Note: GCC = Gulf Cooperation Council; GDP = gross domestic product; OIC = Oil importing country; OEC = Developing oil exporting country.

will fund ICT investments in developing MENA, and nearly two-thirds of this expenditure will be spent on maintenance projects (table 2.7).

Annual water and sanitation expenditure needs amount to US$4.9 billion per year, or 0.3 percent of regional GDP, with US$2.9 billion needed to meet demand for water and sanitation services in urban areas (see table 2.8). The Millennium Development Goals (MDGs) were taken into account when estimating the investment needs for water and sanitation.

Table 2.9   Access Shortfall Compared to MDG Linear Path Achievement
percentage points

	Urban areas		Rural areas	
Country/economy	Water	Sanitation	Water	Sanitation
Oil importing country				
Djibouti		19.7	28.2	54.8
Jordan	1.4	0.7	3.2	
Morocco		4.8	11.2	1.3
Tunisia		0.8		0.2
West Bank and Gaza	9	2.6		4.6
Oil exporting country				
Algeria	15	1.4	13.3	
Iran, Islamic Rep.	0.7	4.1	3.3	5.8
Iraq	7.1	6.9	9.2	
Libya	1.8	1.1	2.6	1.4
Syrian Arab Republic	3.4	0.2	0	
Yemen, Rep.	19.5		14.6	6.8
GCC				
Kuwait	0.4		0.4	
Oman		1.1	5.1	0.7
Saudi Arabia	1.1		0.1	
United Arab Emirates		0.7		1.8

Source: World Bank data.
Note: GCC = Gulf Cooperation Council; MDG = Millennium Development Goal. There are no data available for rural sanitation for Saudi Arabia. A blank space means the country is on track to achieve the relevant MDG.

Analyzing trends in access to these services show that most countries are behind schedule in achieving these by 2015—only Egypt and Qatar are on track. Table 2.9 shows the access shortfall by country and country group, defined as additional access, which should have been completed by 2008, if countries were following a linear achievement path toward the MDGs.

Potential of Infrastructure Investment in Boosting Employment

This section provides a first-round assessment of the extent to which infrastructure activities could play a role in speeding up job creation and resolving MENA's employment problem. It presents employment shares by infrastructure sector and country and compares those to international benchmarks. The data used in this section summarize the information that can be computed based on the sectoral disaggregation of employment following the international standard industrial classification (ISIC) of sectors, allowing an identification of electricity and water sector jobs as well as jobs in transport and communication sectors.[7] These activities add up to what is usually defined as infrastructure in the sector. In spite of the limited ability to unbundle employment into subsector specific details, these data prove extremely useful as they allow identification of jobs associated with the delivery of electricity and water services as well as a really good approximation of jobs in transport and communication services.

Data on construction are included in this section as an important element of infrastructure investment.[8] The construction category encompasses housing and building construction. These two activities are likely to be the main drivers of job creation, but other infrastructure investments are still likely to account for a significant share of employment creation.

The infrastructure and construction sectors in the region employ approximately 18.2 million people—10.6 million in construction and 7.6 million in infrastructure. About 2.2 million of these jobs are in the GCC economies, 9.2 million in other MENA OECs, and 6.8 million in the MENA OICs. On average, jobs in the infrastructure sector represent around 8.0 percent of the employment in the region, whereas construction jobs constitute around 11.3 percent (table 2.10).

OECs have a higher share of jobs in the infrastructure and construction sectors, not only relative to other groups in the region but also to international benchmarks. In contrast, oil importers' employment shares are more in line with international averages, although their employment in infrastructure is below various international benchmarks (table 2.10). It is worth noting that many of the infrastructure and construction jobs in the GCC economies are performed by migrant workers, although lack of data precludes separating the impact of infrastructure investments on employment of migrant and national workers.

Table 2.10   Employment Shares of Infrastructure and Construction Sectors
Percentage of all employed in 2009

	Infrastructure services share of total employment	Construction share of total employment	Total infrastructure services and construction share
GCC	5.8	12.0	17.7
OECs	9.6	13.0	22.6
OICs	7.1	9.4	16.5
Total for MENA	8.0	11.3	19.3
World average	7.7	8.4	16.1
Developed countries	7.2	8.2	15.4
Developing countries	7.6	8.6	16.2

Sources: World Bank and ILO data.
Note: GCC = Gulf Cooperation Council; MENA = Middle East and North Africa; OEC = developing oil exporting country; OIC = oil importing country.

Assuming that world benchmarks gauge the normal size of employment in the infrastructure sector (table 2.10), we conclude that in general there is limited scope for infrastructure activities to speed up job creation. In the OECs, infrastructure's share in total employment is much higher than the world average, so the scope for increasing the relative size of employment in the sector is limited. The same is the case with employment in construction in all subregions and the region as a whole, although there is some scope to expand the relative size of employment in infrastructure services in oil importing and GCC countries, where infrastructure's employment share is below world norms.

Within infrastructure, the transport and communication sectors are the most labor intensive, employing about 7 percent of all employed, compared to approximately 1 percent in electricity and water sectors (table 2.11). This means that in 2009, the electricity and water sectors in the region relied on a labor force of about 1 million workers, whereas transport and communications employed approximately 6.5 million workers. GCC's employment levels within infrastructure are significantly lower than international averages. In contrast, developing oil exporters have a significantly larger employment share in the transport and communication subsector than that of other countries. Their employment shares in the electricity and water sectors are consistent with those of other regions, and there is some scope for an increase when compared with the average standards of developing countries.

These aggregate numbers hide significant variations across economies. For example, figure 2.3 shows that the Islamic Republic of Iran is an outlier in terms of employment in the construction sector as it employs almost four times as many workers as the regional average. Egypt and Saudi Arabia stand out as the only two economies employing more workers in the infrastructure sector than in the construction sector.

Table 2.11   Infrastructure Jobs by Sector in MENA
percent

	Electricity and water	Transport and communication
GCC economies (GCC)	0.8	4.9
Developing oil exporting countries (OECs)	1.1	8.5
Oil importing countries (OICs)	1.1	6.0
Total for MENA	1.1	6.9
Developed countries	0.9	6.3
Developing countries	1.2	6.6

Source: Based on ILO data.
Note: GCC = Gulf Cooperation Council; MENA = Middle East and North Africa.

Figure 2.3   Shares of Infrastructure and Construction Jobs in Total Employment in MENA

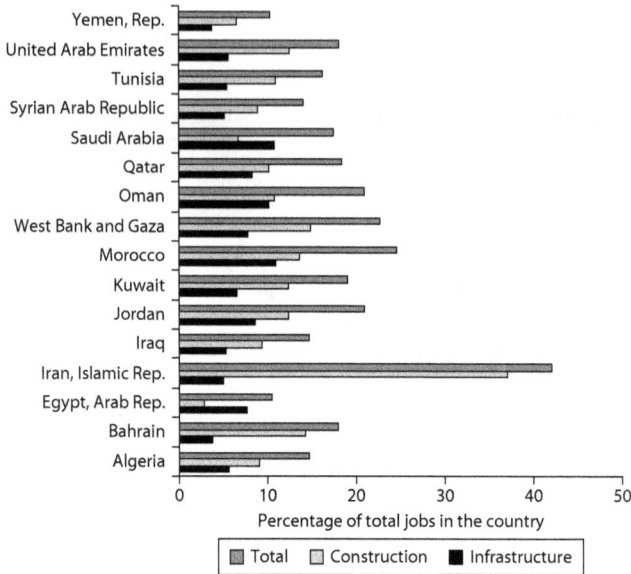

Source: Based on ILO data.
Note: MENA = Middle East and North Africa.

This overview of the relative importance of the infrastructure-related sectors for employment in the region provides a reality check. It suggests that investment in infrastructure alone will not solve the employment problem in the region. According to the employment estimates discussed in this chapter, the infrastructure sector would have to increase its employment by more than 20 percent every year to meet the overall annual job creation target of the region. Such a high rate of growth is difficult to sustain over the long run, given the already large relative size of employment in infrastructure and construction in the region.

However, infrastructure investments can certainly play a significant role in efforts to create jobs in the region. Annual infrastructure investment and maintenance needs through 2020 are estimated to be $106 billion or 6.9 percent of the regional GDP. OECs have the highest demand, representing 46 percent of the regional needs, and they will need to commit almost 11 percent of their GDP annually to keep up with their economic and demographic growth. The needs of the OICs and the GCC economies are smaller at 6 and 5 percent of GDP, respectively. Next, chapters 3 and 4 discuss the implications of infrastructure investment for employment creation in the short and medium run, respectively.

Annex 2A Econometric Models for Infrastructure Needs

Method	Paved roads Probit for grouped data	Total roads Fixed effects	Rail lines Fixed effects	Ports Fixed effects	Telephone mainlines Logit for grouped data	Mobile lines Logit for grouped data	Electricity generation Fixed effects
Per capita GDP	-0.261***	0.111*	-0.0107	1.124***	0.983***	0.414***	0.652***
	(0.00189)	(0.0575)	(0.0422)	(0.1640)	(0.0002)	(0.0002)	(0.0549)
Share of manufactures in GDP	0.131***	0.00209	-0.0428	0.152	0.0686***	-0.142***	0.199***
	(0.0018)	(0.0435)	(0.0395)	(0.1110)	(0.0002)	(0.0002)	(0.0343)
Share of agriculture in GDP	-0.179***	-0.0772	0.0630	-0.202*	0.199***	0.184***	0.147***
	(0.0020)	(0.0491)	(0.0393)	(0.1210)	(0.0002)	(0.0002)	(0.0429)
Population density	-0.574***	-0.427***	-0.929***	0.409	-0.000914***	2.133***	-0.00847
	(0.0046)	(0.1160)	(0.1020)	(0.2980)	(0.0003)	(0.00034)	(0.1000)
Urbanization	-0.493***	0.377***	-0.0421	0.279	3.361***	1.259***	0.141
	(0.0054)	(0.1370)	(0.1120)	(0.3370)	(0.0005)	(0.0005)	(0.0872)
Population growth	n.a.	n.a.	n.a.	n.a.	-1.645***	-0.828***	n.a.
					(0.0013)	(0.0016)	
Time trend	0.0985***	-5.684	-1.224	n.a.	n.a.	n.a.	0.0697***
	(0.0005)	(4.1460)	(1.3040)				(0.0126)
Time trend squared	n.a.	0.00714	0.00155	n.a.	n.a.	n.a.	n.a.
		(0.0052)	(0.0016)				
Market age	n.a.	n.a.	n.a.	0.102***	0.107***	0.111***	n.a.
				(0.0121)	(0.0092)	(0.0114)	
Market age squared	n.a.	n.a.	n.a.	-0.00117***	-0.00366***	0.00414***	n.a.
				(0.0002)	(0.0034)	(0.0052)	
Constant	-35.32***	1,128	236.2	-15.28***	-8.373***	-13.74***	-34.94***
	(0.1910)	(828.6600)	(260.0000)	(2.0940)	(0.0028)	(0.00289)	(4.7220)
Observations	a	633	551	496	a	a	1,034
R^2		0.119	0.540	0.801			0.4590
Number of coefficients	172	172	109	102			173

Source: Ianchovichina et al. 2012.

Note: GDP = gross domestic product. Standard errors in parentheses. All relevant variables are in logarithms.

a. indicates a large number of observations due to the grouped technique.

n.a. = not applicable.

*$p < .1$ **$p < .05$ ***$p < .01$

Annex 2B Data Sources and Descriptions Used for Model of Investment Requirements

Gross domestic product (GDP) in constant 2000 US$ is taken from the World Development Indicators (WDI) database of the World Bank (http://data.worldbank.org/) and the United Nations (UN) National Accounts Main Aggregates Database (http://unstats.un.org/unsd /snaama/selbasicFast.asp). GDP projections for all MENA economies except for West Bank and Gaza come from the World Bank Growth Forecasting Tool described in Ianchovichina and Kacker (2005).

Shares of value added in agriculture and manufacturing come from the WDI database of the World Bank (http://data.worldbank.org/) and UN National Accounts Main Aggregates Database (http://unstats.un.org /unsd/snaama/selbasicFast.asp).

Total and urban population data are taken from the WDI database of the World Bank (http://data.worldbank.org/). Projections are obtained from the UN World Urbanization Prospects (2009 revision) (http:// esa.un.org/unpd/wup/index.htm).

Containerization, measured as the total number of trafficking containers, is obtained from the WDI database of the World Bank (http://data. worldbank.org/) and harmonized with the Containerization International Yearbook (1970–2006), published by Containerization International (http://www.ci-online.co.uk).

Telephone lines, mobile phones (in subscribers per 1,000 inhabitants), *paved and total roads,* and *rail lines* (in thousands of kilometers) come from the WDI database of the World Bank (http://data .worldbank.org/).

Electricity generating capacity, in millions of kilowatts, is taken from the U.S. Energy Information Administration, (http://tonto.eia.doe.gov /cfapps/ipdbproject/IEDIndex3.cfm?tid=2&pid=2&aid=12).

Electrification rate, measured as the fraction of population with access to electricity, is obtained from World Energy Outlook 2006, 2009, and 2010 published by the International Energy Agency (http://www .worldenergyoutlook.org/).

Access to improved water and sanitation in urban and rural areas is defined as the fraction of total population with access to these services. It is taken from the WDI database of the World Bank (http://data .worldbank.org/).

Waste water treatment, measured as the fraction of the population connected to public waste water treatment plants, is obtained from the UN Statistical Division (http://unstats.un.org/unsd/environment/wastewater.htm).

Kilometers of total and paved roads and port traffic in tons for Oman are obtained from the Ministry of National Economy (http://www.moneoman.gov.om/Stat_Online_desp.aspx).

Electrification rate for Djibouti is taken from the energy survey that was carried out by the government and the World Bank (http://www.ministere-finances.dj/statistiques/Projets/rapportfinalenergie.pdf).

Annex 2C Data Imputations

In the absence of data for a sector or subsector in a country, regional averages of investment as percent of GDP were imputed to obtain total investment needs. Table 2C.1 shows the economies and sectors for which regional averages were imputed.

Table 2C.1   Imputation of Average Investment as Percent of GDP When Data Were Not Available

Sector	Economies
Transport	
Paved roads	Syrian Arab Republic
Unpaved roads	Syrian Arab Republic
Ports	Bahrain, Iraq, Libya, Qatar, Syrian Arab Republic, and West Bank and Gaza
Electricity	
Electricity (access)	West Bank and Gaza
Water and sanitation	
Water, rural areas	Bahrain
Sanitation, rural areas	Bahrain and Saudi Arabia

Note: GDP = gross domestic product.

Notes

1. All the labor data are extracted from the International Labour Organization (ILO) database, published on their website. Upon request, additional data were provided by ILO staff. Data after 2008 are projections and not measurements.

2. In some cases, recent trends of annual growth of the same series are used to fill in missing values. United Nations National Accounts Main Aggregates Database is used for historical GDP and for the value-added components of

agriculture and manufacturing. Additional data on container port traffic is taken from the Containerization International Yearbook (1970–2006). Extra information on roads and paved roads is available for Oman. GDP projections are from the World Bank.

3. When past growth rates were not available, a Hodrick-Prescott filter (with a smoothing factor of 100) was used to obtain the long-run growth rate trend of the past 10 years (1999–2009), resulting in an implied annual growth rate equivalent to that of the World Bank projections. Growth rates are then used to obtain 2010–20 GDP scenarios.

4. Per capita stocks of infrastructure are regressed against per capita income, the share of GDP derived from agriculture and manufacturers, demographic density, and urbanization rate. Time dummies and country fixed effects are used to proxy differences in infrastructure prices. In the case of telecommunications and ports, a market-age variable accounts for the speed of technological change across countries, that is, mobile penetration and adoption of containerization. Lagged dependant variables are included to eliminate the structural part of interest. Analysis of spurious regressions have been made in these studies showing that a structure of lagged variables as in Arellano and Bond estimations can eliminate all variance thus eliminating the structural part of interest (Yepes, Pierce, and Foster 2008).

5. This model is a simplified version of the Highway Design and Maintenance Standards Model developed by the World Bank.

6. As there is no available information on road quality in the MENA countries, global average quality levels are used as in Ianchovichina et al. (2012). Although reaching 100 percent of good quality is an unrealistic goal, the estimation of investment needs is based on demand. A road is expected to deliver the service for which it was built, despite the fact that it could actually perform at lower quality. Operation at lower quality represents either the accumulation of a larger liability in terms of rehabilitation or costs internalized by users.

7. The data are from the ILO tables 4b and 4c, which disaggregate employment into industrial sectors at the 1-digit level, according to the more recent ISIC of economic activities; Revision 3 (1990) in 4b and Revision 2 (1968) in 4c. The ILO sector E covers two sectors: electricity, gas, steam, and hot water supply (sector 40, ISIC); and collection, purification, and distribution of water (sector 41, ISIC). ILO's sector I covers five ISIC categories: land transport; transport via pipelines (sector 60, ISIC); water transport (sector 61, ISIC); air transport (sector 62, ISIC); supporting and auxiliary transport activities and activities of travel agencies (sector 63, ISIC); and post and telecommunications (sector 64, ISIC).

8. ILO's sector E matches the ISIC sector covering construction (sector 45, ISIC).

References

Fay, M., and T. Yepes. 2003. "Investing in Infrastructure: What Is Needed from 2000 to 2010." World Bank Policy Research Working Paper 3102, World Bank, Washington DC.

Ianchovichina, E., and P. Kracker. 2005. "Growth Trends in the Developing World: Country Forecasts and Determinants." World Bank Policy Research Working Paper 3775. World Bank, Washington DC.

Ianchovichina, E., A. Estache, R. Foucart, G. Garsous, and T. Yepes. 2012. "Job Creation through Infrastructure Investment in the Middle East and North Africa." Policy Research Working Paper No. 6164, World Bank, Washington, DC.

World Bank. 2004. *Unlocking the Employment Potential in the Middle East and North Africa*. Washington, DC: World Bank.

Yepes, T., J. Pierce, and V. Foster. 2008. "Making Sense of Sub-Saharan Africa's Infrastructure Endowment: A Benchmarking Approach." Africa Infrastructure Country Diagnostic Working Paper No. 1, World Bank, Washington, DC.

CHAPTER 3

Short-Run Employment Effects of Infrastructure Investment

The cost of creating a job is a crucial factor when assessing the potential of infrastructure investments in creating employment. This cost varies across sectors, making expenditure in certain areas more job intensive than in others. The cost of job creation also varies across countries; a given expenditure can create many more jobs in one country than in another.

This chapter describes different methods for assessing the employment generating potential of infrastructure investments in the short run. The next three sections present the application of different approaches toward assessing the short-term employment effects of infrastructure investments in the Middle East and North Africa (MENA) region. The last section discusses the implications of using labor-intensive technologies in the maintenance of unpaved roads.

Techniques for Estimating the Cost of a Job and the Employment Generated by Investment in Infrastructure

Employment generated by infrastructure spending is typically assessed in two steps. First, direct employment is estimated using information on the nature of infrastructure spending and the amount of different types of labor required by financed projects. Second, indirect and induced employment effects are estimated using multipliers from past experience that link these types of employment to direct employment.

To estimate direct employment a given investment project would create, it is necessary to start with actual data from a similar infrastructure project. The ratio of jobs generated to investment expenditure can then be used directly or with some adjustments to produce estimates in cases where actual data are not available. The accounting identity connecting output to its component parts represents the link between investment spending and the employment generated by this investment (Scottish Government 2011):

Output at basic prices = Total domestic purchases at basic prices + Imports + Taxes on products + Compensation of employees + Gross operating surplus.

The output at basic prices corresponds to the amount spent on a project. Total domestic purchases at basic prices correspond to the purchase of inputs from all sectors of the economy. Imports are items financed by the investment and purchased directly from abroad. Taxes on products include items, such as property taxes, capital, and payroll taxes. The compensation of employees is the total payment to labor for producing the output, including wages and other nonwage benefits, such as insurance and other benefits. The gross operating surplus is the remainder accruing to companies for their production.

The total compensation of employees covers various full-time and part-time jobs paying different wage rates. The simplest approach to link total expenditure of a project to the direct employment it creates is to divide total employee compensation by the average annual wage plus benefits for the sector, to produce an estimate of the number of full-time equivalent (FTE) employees.[1] This estimate provides a simple link between expenditure and direct jobs, that is, the employment multiplier.

A more detailed approach would be (1) to categorize jobs by skill levels, for example, skilled, semiskilled, and unskilled; (2) to assign to each level the average wage plus benefits for that skill level; and (3) finally, to identify the number of FTE employees in each group, so that the sum of the number of FTE employees in each skill group times their average wage is equal to total employee compensation (Schwartz, Andres, and Dragoiu 2009). This would provide three ratios between expenditure and the employment types, or three employment multipliers for the respective skill levels.

The employment multipliers for an actual project can be used to obtain an estimate of direct employment generated by expenditure associated with a similar project. There are two main sources of information that provide evidence on employment multipliers. Project-level data that may have been collected could give evidence on expenditures and employment creation (REPP 2001). Project-level data have the advantage of referring to a specific type of investment and, in cases where the projection is required for exactly the same type of investment, these data will provide the most reliable projection of likely employment. The accuracy of the projection declines with increase in the discrepancy between the proposed and the specific investment project.

In many cases, project-level data are not available or are available only for a specific technology or project that differs substantially from the one that needs to be assessed. In these cases, the usual practice is to use data from an input-output (IO) table (CH2MHILL 2009). The IO table, if available, provides for each sector of the economy the average expenditure on each input required to produce a unit of output of that sector. As this includes total employee compensation, it can be used to connect total expenditure and expenditure on employment in that sector. The IO table needs to be supplemented by national data on sector wages or employment in order to convert the employee compensation figure to an employment figure per unit of expenditure. This ratio can then be applied to future potential expenditures to generate an estimate of associated employment.[2]

The direct employment effect understates, in some instances significantly, the total employment generated by infrastructure spending. In some instances, the sum of indirect plus induced jobs created by infrastructure spending has been estimated to be of comparable magnitude to the number of direct jobs created by this investment. In the United States, six different types of highway projects had type II multipliers[3] averaging 1.9, whereas a transmission line power project had a type II multiplier of 1.7 (Babcock et al. 2010; Pfeifenberger et al. 2010). A study on Malaysia by Bekhet (2011) found type II multipliers to be 3.5 for investments in the electricity and gas sectors, 2.4 for water works and supply, and 1.7 for building and construction. A study on the Egyptian 2008/09 stimulus package (ILO 2010) reported infrastructure type II multipliers ranging between 1.2 for investments in water and sewage and 1.6 for investments in construction and building. These and other results in the literature indicate that in addition to direct effects, it is desirable to estimate indirect and induced employment effects of an infrastructure project.

Type I and type II multipliers can be derived from IO tables, using the Leontief inverse that enables the calculation of the costs associated with the production of extra output in a given sector by factoring in all the inputs required (directly and indirectly) for its production. As with the direct employment multiplier, it is necessary to convert employee compensation in each sector into employment, using sector-level wage plus benefit rates. Once total employment generated by an initial investment is estimated, it is possible to calculate the cost of creating a single job. Box 3.1 presents a discussion of the strengths and weaknesses of using IO tables for generating employment estimates. Many countries do not have IO tables, but hybrid methods, such as those pioneered by Schwartz, Andres, and Dragoiu (2009) and by LECG (2009), can be adapted to address transferability across countries at different times and stages of development.

Hybrid Approaches to Estimating the Short-Term Employment Effects of Infrastructure Investment

Hybrid approaches work best in those cases where economies have similar structures and are at similar levels of development. Hybrid approaches for estimating employment generated by infrastructure investment can have two components—*limited* hybrid case and *full* hybrid case. In the limited hybrid case, direct employment generated by investment in a country may be available from project-level data for the same country. Indirect and induced employment are derived using multipliers from another country where there is an IO table (see Schwartz, Andres, and Dragoiu 2009). In the full hybrid case, there would be no relevant data for a certain country, and all information, including the link from expenditure to direct, indirect, and induced employment, has to be taken from data available for another country.

An important factor that must be recognized while making comparisons over time or across countries is that labor costs vary in nominal terms. High labor costs will translate into high overall costs of creating a job or equivalently one needs to recognize that a given nominal expenditure in a sector generates less employment (direct and indirect) at higher wages. Assuming a constant wage rate across a group of countries, as in Schwartz, Andres, and Dragoiu (2009), might be acceptable when one needs to obtain an aggregate number for a group of countries. However, a calculation of country-level employment figures based on regional

Box 3.1

Pros and Cons of Input-Output Table Use for Generating Employment Estimates

Strengths

The major advantage of using input-output (IO) tables for generating employment estimates is that they make it possible to calculate not only direct but also indirect and induced employment. Project-based data can be used to generate only direct employment estimates.

The IO approach is well suited for estimating employment effects of large sector programs that reflect the existing mix of projects because sectors in IO tables tend to be broad aggregates, including energy, water, and sewage, or roads.

Although IO tables are often out-of-date by several years, studies have shown that changes in IO tables over a decade make only small differences to employment multipliers.

Weaknesses

For projects that are not typical of the sector mix, the IO coefficient could result in misleading estimates of employment generated by a given amount of investment.

The labor intensity for a particular project could be higher or lower than the sector average, and the use of indirect employment could be quite different from the sector average. For example, the scale of a project could affect labor intensity so that the sector average would not represent a project at the particular scale required.

The use of the employment multiplier implies that the wage associated with a potential project is equal to the average wage rate for that sector. This assumption may not be accurate in cases where there is considerable wage variation and may bias the estimates of the employed and the induced employment resulting from consumption financed by employee compensation.

IO models do not incorporate potentially important supply constraints. Employment may not be able to respond to demand. Large-scale investments run the risk of creating a "crowding out" effect with employment increasing in the target sector but decreasing elsewhere. These concerns are most relevant for large projects in countries with tight labor markets.

average wages could differ substantially from the one based on country-specific wages.[4]

Given these issues, adjustments have to be made to values taken from IO tables that reflect wage rate changes over time and wage differences across countries. Adjustments are required when there are differences between the year of the IO table calculation and the year of the investment-generated employment estimate. Adjustments are also required when values have to be imported from one country with an IO table to another without an IO table.

The general level of wages can be indexed by gross domestic product (GDP) per capita in nominal terms to correct for increases in per capita income and income differences across countries, as suggested by LECG (2009). Using data from Gardiner and Theobald (2010)[5] and regressing the hourly construction wage, inclusive of benefits, on GDP per capita, both expressed in 2009 US$ (table 3.1), one can show that wages are highly and positively correlated to GDP per capita. This result provides evidence that the approach of scaling down one country's wages by the ratio of its GDP per capita to another country's GDP per capita is a good approximation to wages in the other country. The adjustment, however, would not be sufficient in cases where individual sector wages change relative to the general wage rate. It is worth noting that correcting employment generated in every sector by the same factor will reduce the estimated number of jobs created (direct, type I, and type II), but will not alter the values of the type I and type II multipliers.

A third correction in the process of deriving the direct employment calculation involves the conversion of national data on basic wage rates to gross rates, including benefits. Gardiner and Theobald (2010) provide data for the basic wage in the construction sector and a total labor cost basis for a number of countries, including the Arab Republic of Egypt. Table 3.2 indicates that for Egypt, the ratio of basic to total wages increases slightly with the skill level and varies between 0.83 and 0.88. The ratio for semiskilled workers is taken as an estimate of the differential between basic and total wages for all infrastructure employees.

Table 3.1   Regression of Semiskilled Hourly Construction Wage on GDP per Capita

	Coefficient	t-statistic
Intercept	1.15	0.54
GDP per capita	0.00084	12.0
Goodness of fit	$R^2 = 0.85$	n.a.

Sources: Gardiner and Theobald 2010; World Development Indicators; World Bank data.
Note: GDP = gross domestic product; n.a. = not applicable.

Table 3.2   Construction Sector Hourly Wages in the Arab Republic of Egypt, January 2009

US$

	Unskilled	Semiskilled	Skilled
Basic rate	0.88	1.06	1.25
Total rate	1.06	1.25	1.42
Ratio	0.83	0.85	0.88

Source: Gardiner and Theobald 2009.

Although the adjustment by GDP per capita attempts to correct for differences in labor costs, there may also be substantial differences in the production structure of economies. Thus, an IO table for one country may not be representative of the true IO structure of another country. It is also likely that the larger the difference between per capita GDP levels of two countries, the greater the difference in the IO structures. More importantly, resource endowments tend to have a large effect on the structure of production even at similar levels of income per capita. So it is expected that the IO table of a major developing oil exporting country (OEC) would differ substantially from the IO table of an oil importing country (OIC).

Estimating the Cost of Creating Jobs in Oil Importing MENA Countries

The availability of non-OECD countries' IO tables with employment and multiplier data is limited. Three relevant studies discussing employment data from an IO table are described in table 3.3. The case of Malaysia is the least relevant to MENA due to the country's high income level. South Africa's case is more relevant as its income level is closer to that of developing MENA. Still, both studies rely on outdated IO tables[6] that do not contain information on direct employment as a separate category. The study on Egypt (ILO 2010) is the most pertinent for the estimation undertaken in this study.[7] Egypt's IO table is the most recent. It has been upgraded to include 22 sectors based on International Labour Organization (ILO) data for 2007/08 (ILO 2010). The IO table has other big advantages. Egypt's construction sector is disaggregated into five subsectors, corresponding to areas favored by the fiscal stimulus of 2009 that might be favored in future infrastructure packages in the region. Information on sector wages has been integrated with sector employee compensation data to provide an employment estimate. The calculation of type I and type II multipliers has also been carried out for all the sectors.[8] Finally, the structure of Egypt's economy is relatively similar to the structure of other MENA OICs.

Table 3.3   Sector Coverage Provided by Various Input-Output Tables

	Egypt, Arab Rep.	*South Africa*	*Malaysia*
Year of IO table	2007/08	2003	2000
GDP per capita, 2009 US$	2,270	5,764	7,030
Categories of employment identified	Direct, indirect, induced	Direct, indirect, induced	Direct + indirect + induced, direct + indirect
Infrastructure sectors identified	Construction Buildings Roads and bridges Water and sewage Electricity stations Other construction Electricity Transport and communications	Electricity and gas Water Construction Communication services Transport services	Electricity and gas Water works and supply Building and construction Transport and communications

Sources: Bekhet 2011 for Malaysia; International Labour Organization 2010 for Arab Republic of Egypt; Tregenna 2007 for South Africa.
Note: GDP = gross domestic product; IO = input-output.

Bearing this consideration in mind, the study uses Egypt's IO table and multipliers to make calculations for the six MENA OICs whose 2009 GDP per capita in US$ is shown in brackets: Djibouti (1,214), Egypt (2,270), Jordan (4,212), Lebanon (8,175), Morocco (2,811), and Tunisia (3,792).[9] The Gulf Cooperation Council (GCC) and OECs were judged to be too different in terms of economic structure and GDP per capita levels to make extrapolations from the Egyptian case reliable.

In addition to the five construction activities, information is available on two other broad infrastructure sectors: electricity, and transport and communications (table 3.3). These broad sectors include all types of projects and activities carried out during the year for which the table was constructed, apart from construction in electricity. For example, the electricity sector would include wages paid for operations and maintenance (O&M) during the year in question. Transport and communications is even broader and would include construction in the communications sector.

One can estimate the cost of a job in Egypt in 2009 for each of these sectors based on the employment (type I and type II) multipliers for 2007/08 in the Egyptian IO table. Table 3.4 presents values in US$ for the cost of creating one direct job, one direct or indirect job (type I), and one direct, indirect, or induced job (type II). The data for calculating the costs of a job (direct, type I, or type II) are taken from ILO (2010). Sector wages are adjusted for nonwage benefits and sector employee

Table 3.4 Cost of Creating a Job in Selected Infrastructure Sectors in the Arab Republic of Egypt, 2009

	Share of employee compensation (%)	Average annual total wage in 2007/08 (LE)	Cost of type II job in 2007/08 (LE)	Cost of direct job in 2009 (US$)	Cost of type I job in 2009 (US$)	Cost of type II job in 2009 (US$)	M(I)	M(II)
Electricity	20.8	20,562	65,360	21,700	20,472	14,564	1.06	1.49
Construction								
Building	8.2	5,838	49,020	17,805	13,092	10,924	1.36	1.63
Roads, bridges	13.3	1,698	11,765	2,858	2,774	2,621	1.03	1.09
Water, sewage	14.7	4,872	27,360	7,376	6,831	6,096	1.08	1.23
Electricity stations	5.2	3,574	51,151	15,387	13,040	11,398	1.18	1.35
Others	23.3	16,548	43,573	15,632	13,247	9,709	1.18	1.61
Transport and communications	13.5	19,140	78,432	31,808	23,738	17,476	1.34	1.82

Sources: ILO 2010 and World Bank data.
Note: M(I) = type I multiplier; M(II) = type II multiplier.

compensation. Adjustment to 2009 levels was carried out by allowing for growth in GDP per capita over the period from 2007/08 to 2009 and using the official exchange rate in 2009 to convert to US$. The most relevant figures when considering a large-scale program are the costs of creating type II jobs as these give the upper limit to the short-run number of jobs created by a given amount of spending, and hence a lower limit to the cost per job.

The cost of creating a job in the Egyptian construction sector varies substantially depending on the type of construction activity. The cost of a new job is the lowest when constructing roads and bridges and the highest when constructing buildings. For some sectors, such as roads and bridges, the costs of a type I job (and of a type II job) are not much lower than the costs of a direct job. By contrast, in the transport and communications sector, the cost of a direct job is considerably higher than the cost of a type I job or a type II job. The differences in the costs of creating different types of jobs are explained in part by differences in sector wages, but in all cases these are only a minor fraction of the total costs. The multipliers are generally quite small, and even in the largest case of transport and communications, the type II multiplier is substantially lower than that used by Schwartz, Andres, and Dragoiu (2009).

A comparison of these costs with those found in other studies, and obtained either based on calculations from IO tables or project data, helps to place these figures in a broader perspective (table 3.5). Such a comparison is not a straightforward task because other studies give results for different sectors and time periods, and not all categories of jobs are presented in every case. Apart from the IO-based estimates from Tregenna (2007), DIT (2007), Bekhet (2011), and the U.S. studies quoted by Schwartz, Andres, and Dragoiu (2009), the comparison includes studies based on World Bank projects in which direct employment estimates were made. Where possible numbers have been adjusted by the growth in GDP per capita and converted to dollars to provide estimates of the cost of jobs in 2009 in US$. These costs per job are used to calculate the number of jobs that would be generated per billion dollars of spending in the sector—the metric commonly used in studies on the employment effects of infrastructure investment.

The estimated costs of a job shown in table 3.5 need to be interpreted with two considerations in mind. First, the cost of one direct job may be considerably greater than the cost of one type II job, as shown also in annex 3A and box 3A.1. Second, the costs are expected to vary with the level of GDP per capita, and several of the countries included are at

Table 3.5 Cost of Creating Infrastructure-Related Jobs by Country
2009 US$

Country	Source	Sector	Category of employment	Cost per job	Jobs per $ billion
Argentina	Schwartz et al.	Highways	Direct	606,060	1,600
Armenia	Ishihara & Bennett	Lifeline roads improvement	Direct	30,400	33,000
Brazil	Schwartz et al.	Roads	Direct	60,325	17,000
	Schwartz et al.	Rain drainage networks	Direct	29,411	34,000
	Schwartz et al.	Sewerage	Direct	45,981	22,000
	Schwartz et al.	Hydropower	Direct	222,222	4,500
Bangladesh	World Bank	Rural transport improvement	Direct	4,412	227,000
Colombia	Schwartz et al.	Local roads	Direct	44,444	23,000
	Schwartz et al.	Feeder roads	Direct	27,907	36,000
Colombia	Schwartz et al.	Expansion of water and sanitation networks	Direct	10,000	100,000
Georgia	Vesin	International roads	Direct	58,824	17,000
	Vesin	Secondary and local roads	Direct	50,000	20,000
Honduras	Schwartz et al.	Water captation	Direct	23,077	43,000
	Schwartz et al.	Rehabilitation of water networks	Direct	17,143	58,000
	Schwartz et al.	Expansion of water networks	Direct	15,000	67,000
	Schwartz et al.	New treatment plant	Direct	40,000	25,000
India	DIT	ICT—hardware	Direct	19,452	51,000
	DIT	ICT—software	Direct	9,214	108,000
Mexico/Guatemala/Peru[a]	Vesin	Rural road maintenance	Direct	2,000–5,000	500,000–200,000

(continued next page)

Table 3.5 *(continued)*

Country	Source	Sector	Category of employment	Cost per job	Jobs per $ billion
Malaysia	Bekhet	Electricity and gas	Type II	57,381	17,000
	Bekhet	Water works & supply	Type II	27,003	37,000
	Bekhet	Building and construction	Type II	15,829	63,000
	Bekhet	Transport	Type II	20,866	48,000
	Bekhet	Communications	Type II	51,005	20,000
Peru	Schwartz et al.	Rural electrification	Direct	43,478	23,000
South Africa	Tregenna	Electricity and gas	Type II	27,375	37,000
	Tregenna	Water	Type II	31,222	32,000
	Tregenna	Construction	Type II	18,452	54,000
	Tregenna	Transport	Type II	31,036	32,000
	Tregenna	Communications	Type II	32,636	31,000
United States	Schwartz et al.	Solar PV	Direct	370,370	2,700
	Schwartz et al.	Wind power	Direct	294,118	3,400
	Schwartz et al.	Biomass	Direct	1,428,571	700
	Schwartz et al.	Coal-fired generation	Direct	1,333,333	750
	Schwartz et al.	Natural gas–fired generation	Direct	588,235	1,700
Yemen, Rep.[a]	Vesin	Rural roads	Direct	40,000	25,000

Sources: Tregenna 2007; Bekhet 2011; DIT 2007; World Bank 2010; Vesin 2011; Ishihara and Bennett 2010; Schwartz, Andres, and Dragoiu 2009.

Note: ICT = information and communication technology.

a. Indicates that there was insufficient information to update these figures to a 2009 basis.

levels of GDP per capita substantially above that of Egypt or the MENA OICs, whereas India, Bangladesh, and Honduras are at the low end of the range.

The following patterns can also be detected based on the information in table 3.5. The costs of job creation are strongly linked to the level of GDP per capita, with the highest costs observed in the United States and the lowest in Bangladesh and Mexico/Guatemala/Peru. In certain countries, road programs proved to be low cost, but the nature of the program appears to influence the cost. Costs are high for national road construction programs, whereas local and rural road programs are low cost, and rural road maintenance is least costly. Such low-cost programs may also be "shovel ready" as explained by Ishihara and Bennett (2010). Water and sewage programs appear in the midrange of infrastructure costs, whereas electricity and gas are toward the upper part of the cost range within a country. These findings are similar to those observed in Egypt.

The Egyptian data are used to predict type II job costs in selected MENA countries, using employment multipliers and adjusting for differences in GDP per capita over time and across countries in 2009. The relative costs of jobs in the different sectors are the same across countries, but the general level of job creation costs reflects differences in GDP per capita. Table 3.6 shows the costs of creating type II jobs in six infrastructure sectors of the six OICs, and the wide range in the costs of job creation in the same sector reflects the wide range of GDP per capita found in these six countries. Table 3.7 shows the costs of creating direct jobs in the same set of sectors and countries.

Table 3.6   Estimated Costs of a Type II Job in Six MENA OICs, 2009
US$

| Country | Electricity | Construction | | | | | Transport and communications |
		Building	Roads and bridges	Water and sewage	Electricity stations	Others	
Djibouti	7,789	5,841	1,402	3,260	6,095	5,193	9,347
Egypt, Arab Rep.	14,564	10,924	2,621	6,096	11,398	9,709	17,476
Jordan	27,024	20,268	4,865	11,312	21,149	18,015	32,428
Lebanon	52,449	39,338	9,441	21,955	41,048	34,967	62,940
Morocco	18,035	13,526	3,246	7,549	14,114	12,024	21,642
Tunisia	24,329	18,247	4,379	10,185	19,040	16,219	29,195

Source: World Bank data.

Table 3.7   Estimated Costs of a Direct Job in Six MENA OICs, 2009
US$

| | | Construction | | | | | |
| | | Roads and | Water and | Electricity | | Transport and |
	Electricity	Building	bridges	sewage	stations	Others	communications
Djibouti	11,606	9,522	1,528	3,945	8,229	8,360	17,011
Egypt, Arab Rep.	21,700	17,805	2,858	7,376	15,387	15,632	31,808
Jordan	40,266	33,036	5,302	13,688	28,552	29,006	59,020
Lebanon	78,151	64,120	10,291	26,567	55,414	56,296	114,551
Morocco	26,872	13,526	3,539	9,135	19,054	19,358	39,388
Tunisia	36,251	29,742	4,773	12,324	25,705	26,113	53,135

Source: World Bank data.

Using the estimates in table 3.6, it is possible to derive the number of type II jobs that would be generated by a given expenditure. This number is a rough estimate and has limitations. The number of jobs created depends on availability of suitable labor. Skill shortages will limit the number of jobs that can be created with a given expenditure. This would need to be taken into account in designing the size of any investment program. Even when there are no labor shortages, projects to absorb the investment spending may not be immediately available. Certain types of projects, particularly those that simply scale up existing activities, are more likely to be "shovel ready" than programs focusing on new types of activities.

In cases where there is a need to identify and design projects, there will inevitably be a delay in obtaining substantial employment effects of infrastructure spending. Depending on the internal situation of an economy, a balance may need to be struck between the need to create immediate jobs, possibly in areas where the output of the job itself is of relatively limited value, and the need to create strategic jobs that may take longer to plan and implement. Finally, the calculations reflect adjustments based on 2009 GDP per capita numbers—the latest year for which national accounts data were available. By 2011, GDP per capita is likely to have changed, and where it has increased the cost per job would increase and the number of jobs generated per billion dollars of spending would be lower.

The hybrid approach introduces errors in the estimation of job costs. The closer the economies' structure and behavioral parameters to Egypt's, the better will be the approximation. The accuracy of the estimates also depends on wage levels being proportional to GDP per capita differences between Egypt and a given country, and the similarity of the

Table 3.8   Number of Type II Jobs Generated per US$1 Billion of Spending, 2009

		Construction					Transport and communications
	Electricity	Building	Roads and bridges	Water and sewage	Electricity stations	Others	
Djibouti	86,000	105,000	654,000	254,000	122,000	120,000	59,000
Egypt, Arab Rep.	46,000	56,000	350,000	136,000	65,000	64,000	31,000
Jordan	25,000	30,000	189,000	73,000	35,000	34,000	17,000
Lebanon	13,000	16,000	97,000	38,000	18,000	18,000	9,000
Morocco	37,000	73,900	283,000	109,000	52,000	52,000	25,000
Tunisia	28,000	34,000	210,000	81,000	39,000	38,000	19,000

Source: World Bank data.

mark-up of total wages and benefits over basic wages. The estimation of sector employment is likely to be most accurate when sectors are defined the same way across countries. Results will be biased when sector definitions differ from those available in the Egyptian IO table.

Table 3.8 shows the number of type II jobs created per US$1 billion in each of the six oil importing MENA countries, rounded to the nearest one thousand. Spending on construction of roads and bridges would generate more than twice as many jobs as the same amount of spending in any of the other sectors. Construction of water and sewage infrastructure is the second most job-intensive activity relative to spending, whereas transport and communications is the least job-intensive activity.[10] Because of per capita income differences, spending of a billion dollars generates more than six times as many jobs in a sector in Djibouti as in Lebanon, but the economy of the latter would find it considerably easier to finance the investment expenditure.

Assuming that each country in the oil importing group has the same mixture of investment needs, one can use the estimates of annual new infrastructure needs through 2020 by sector for the oil importing group (table 2.7) to allocate infrastructure spending across sectors and countries. With this information, one can then assess the number of jobs created by a billion dollar infrastructure investment portfolio by country. Because the set of sectors distinguished in table 2.6 and the set of sectors used by the ILO (2010) study on Egypt and presented in table 3.8 are not identical, it is necessary to assign sectors to the narrower range used by the ILO (2010). This allocation is shown in table 3.9.

Estimates of the jobs created in response to US$1 billion infrastructure spending by country and by sector are shown in table 3.10.[11] Egypt, for

Table 3.9   Shares of Total Investment Needs by Sector for OIC
percent

Sector	Share of needs	Sector (ILO basis)	Share of needs
Paved roads	23.4		
Unpaved roads	9.7	Roads	33.1
Rail lines	1.8	Other construction	1.8
Ports	1.9	Building	1.9
Telephone mainlines	3.0		
Mobile lines	10.0	Transport and communications	13.0
Electricity generation	35.3	Electricity stations	35.3
Electricity access	7.2	Electricity	7.2
Water	3.2		
Sanitation	4.4	Water and sanitation	7.6

Source: World Bank data.
Note: ILO = International Labour Organization; OIC = oil importing country.

Table 3.10   Number of Type II Jobs Created by a US$1 Billion Portfolio of Infrastructure Spending

Country	Population (2009)	GDP per capita (2009)	Number of type II jobs
Djibouti	864,000	1,214	291,000
Egypt, Arab Rep.	82,999,000	2,270	155,000
Jordan	5,951,000	4,212	84,000
Lebanon	4,223,000	8,175	43,000
Morocco	31,992,000	2,811	126,000
Tunisia	10,432,000	3,792	93,000
OICs average (population weighted)	136,463,000	2,774	138,000

Sources: WDI; World Bank data.
Note: GDP = gross domestic product; OIC = oil importing country.

instance, is expected to create 155,000 jobs for every US$1 billion spent on infrastructure, whereas the regional average[12] is 138,000 jobs. By contrast, US$1 billion spending on a "prototypical basket of infrastructure investment" in the Latin America and Caribbean (LAC) region is estimated to result in just 80,000 type II jobs, according to Schwartz, Andres, and Dragoiu (2009). The smaller estimate in the LAC region compared to that of OICs in MENA is expected because the average GDP per capita in LAC is more than double that of the MENA OICs. For example, in 2009, LAC's average per capita GDP was $7,260, whereas that of the average OIC was US$2,774. The high value of the type II multiplier assumed by Schwartz, Andres, and Dragoiu (2009) implies that the LAC region's job estimate might be somewhat optimistic.

The assessment of the employment effects of an infrastructure program also needs to consider its duration and nature. A one- or two-year, stimulus-type program would require projects that can be finished within the financing timeframe. Such a program would be associated with the creation of temporary jobs. A more long-term investment program will be associated with projects that have substantial construction, installation, and manufacturing (CIM) components (such as renewable energy projects) and also generate O&M jobs during the life of the new plant. The labor intensity of O&M is usually different from that of CIM, so it would be desirable to make a more detailed analysis of the direct job creation of the various stages of the program, following the approach of REPP (2001). This requires a detailed specification of the nature of investment and follow-up surveys with experienced producers.

Alternative Approaches to Estimating the Short-Term Employment Effects of Infrastructure Spending

The results provided in the previous section are limited to OICs by the need to rely on the Egyptian IO table for representative calculations. By following methods different from the one presented in the previous section, it is possible to come up with estimates of short-term employment effects from infrastructure spending for all three subregions. For example, one can adapt the calculation made for the LAC region by Schwartz, Andres, and Dragoiu (2009) and extend it using calculations from this study.

Schwartz, Andres, and Dragoiu (2009) investigated the employment effects of a stimulus package of spending in various infrastructure sectors in the LAC. They used project data from a number of World Bank studies to derive the share of investment expenditure on labor, and the share going to imports, in the main infrastructure sectors. Combining the expenditure share on labor with data on region-wide average wages (plus benefits) allowed them to compute the direct employment per US$ billion. The authors used data from the U.S. highway sector to derive type I and type II multipliers and calculate indirect and induced employment. Taking a weighted average portfolio of infrastructure sectors allowed them to estimate the employment created by a representative basket of infrastructure investments. Schwartz, Andres, and Dragoiu (2009) estimated that US$1 billion could generate about 40,000 direct and indirect jobs, or 80,000 induced, indirect, and direct jobs. The ratio of type II to type I jobs was notably higher than that found in other studies.

Table 3.11   Estimated Hourly Wages in Infrastructure Works, 2010
US$ per hour

Region	Qualified workers	Nonqualified workers
GCC	4.5	3
OIC	1.5	1
OEC	3.0	2

Source: World Bank data.
Note: GCC = Gulf Cooperation Council; OEC = developing oil exporting country; OIC = oil importing country.

A number of extensions and changes were undertaken to adapt the LAC results to MENA. Wage levels were changed to reflect the fact that wages are not the same in MENA and LAC, but heterogeneous across and within MENA countries. Following the idea of Schwartz, Andres, and Dragoiu (2009), hourly wage costs for construction work are estimated for the three subregions of MENA as given in table 3.11.[13] Computing hourly wages is crucial for all the estimates and is subject to potential underestimation, specifically for the GCC and the OECs. To build our reference values, we have taken data from Gardiner and Theobald[14] (2009) for Lebanon, Qatar, and the United Arab Emirates, and data from Tong (2010) for the the United Arab Emirates.[15] We have adapted these data using the average wage as computed by the ILO's key indicators of the labor market (ILO 2011), and we use homogenous wages within subregions as the investment needs are aggregated values. Our estimates have to be considered carefully as they do not reflect the intensive use of migrant workers in the infrastructure and construction sectors and the high variance of wages in OEC and GCC economies. The share of inputs used in infrastructure projects relevant to MENA countries, but not available from the LAC study, were adapted from other sources (see annex 3B),[16] whereas the investment needs for infrastructure in the MENA region are used as estimated in chapter 2.

Finally, the estimation of the multipliers is reconsidered in order to give a more relevant, but conservative, approximation of potential indirect and induced jobs. The previous section surveys several studies for type II multipliers, indicating an actual employment multiplier effect that ranges between 1.2 and 3.5 and is significantly lower than the estimated multiplier of 4 proposed by Schwartz, Andres, and Dragoiu (2009).[17] The adaptation uses the multipliers for direct job creation as estimated in the previous section, but with a different methodology for calculating the number of direct jobs. A large variance for the hourly wages in the infrastructure sector is described in the previous section.

Figure 3.1   Hourly Wages as a Function of the Share of Labor Inputs in Total Costs

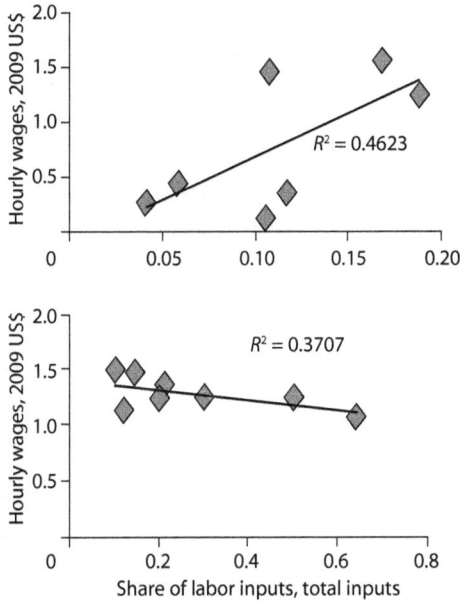

Source: World Bank data.
Note: Top figure displays sector data from the Egyptian IO table. Bottom figure displays data adapted for MENA from Schwartz, Andres, and Dragoiu (2009).

The large variance reflects actual differences across sectors, but these may be less relevant for short-term infrastructure projects. Figure 3.1 illustrates these differences, with the figure on the top showing the positive correlation between sector wages and shares of labor inputs as reconstructed in the Egyptian IO table, and the figure on the bottom showing negative correlation between sector wages and estimated shares of labor inputs adapted from Schwartz, Andres, and Dragoiu (2009). The former is expected in situations where labor and capital are substitutes, whereas the latter is expected when capital and labor are complements.

Table 3.12 summarizes the potential for job creation in the near future in the three subgroups—the GCC, OECs, and OICs. The estimates are obtained based on the various methods presented in this study.[18] The direct jobs, computed from input shares, are in column (1) of table 3.12. Estimates based on multipliers as given in the "Hybrid Approaches to Estimating the Short-Term Employment Effects of Infrastructure Investment" section and the method presented in "Alternative Approaches

Table 3.12   Effect of US$1 Billion of Infrastructure Investment on Job Creation in MENA

	(1)	(2)	(3)
	Direct jobs in infrastructure	Total (from Alternative Approaches to Estimating the Short-Term Employment Effects of Infrastructure Spending Section)	Total (from Hybrid Approaches to Estimating the Short-Term Employment Effects of Infrastructure Investment Section)
GCC countries	20,859	26,194	—
OIC	86,566	109,236	138,000
OEC	39,454	48,573	—
Method and limitations	à la Schwartz et al. (2009) combined with investment needs	Direct jobs from column (1) and multipliers from Hybrid Approaches to Estimating the Short-Term Employment Effects of Infrastructure Investment section	Multipliers and IO table from Egypt, Arab Rep.

Source: World Bank data.
Note: GCC = Gulf Cooperation Council; IO = input-output; MENA = Middle East and North Africa; OEC = developing oil exporting country; OIC = oil importing country; — = not available.

to Estimating the Short-Term Employment Effects of Infrastructure Spending" section are shown in column (2). Estimates using the hybrid method of estimating the cost of creating jobs in OICs are given in column (3). The numbers are calculated based on an investment of US$1 billion, using the infrastructure needs derived in chapter 2.

These results suggest that MENA countries could get a significant boost to job creation through infrastructure investments. Combining the estimates of new jobs created per US$1 billion invested in infrastructure with the estimated investment needs implies total annual job creation of 2.5 million, representing 1.9 percent of the labor force in MENA (table 3.13).

However, actual job creation in response to infrastructure investment programs in the region may not be so large and the following caveats should be kept in mind when using these results for policy discussions. These estimates should be considered the upper bounds for what is possible in the short run as they exclude possible economies of scale and wage increases associated with large, sustained infrastructure investments; leakages in the form of imports; institutional and governance limitations; shortages of certain types of labor; and the type of investment project.

Table 3.13   Estimated Potential Job Creation in Response to Meeting Infrastructure Needs in MENA

	Infrastructure needs (US$ billions)	Direct jobs/ US$ billion	Total jobs[a]/ US$ billion	Labor force (thousands) in 2009	Direct jobs as a share of the labor force (percent)	Total jobs as a share of the labor force (percent)
GCC	15.8	20,859	26,194	16,387	2.01	2.53
OIC	10.3	86,566	109,236	61,598	1.45	1.83
OEC	20.7	39,454	48,573	52,884	1.54	1.90
Total	46.8	2,037,900[b]	2,544,457[b]	130,869	1.56	1.94

Source: World Bank data.

Note: GCC = Gulf Cooperation Council; OEC = developing oil exporting country; OIC = oil importing country.

a. Total jobs include direct, indirect, and induced jobs created per US$1 billion in the short run.

b. The estimate of total direct jobs in the last row of the table refers to the jobs created by meeting annual infrastructure needs. This estimate is obtained by multiplying the estimated infrastructure needs for a particular group with the corresponding direct jobs estimated per US$1 billion, and then summing up across groups.

Certain projects simply scale up existing activities, and new projects may not have immediate employment impact as there is considerable investment in planning and design.

The sectoral distribution of investment would also affect the number of jobs created. There are large differences between sectors' potential to create jobs through infrastructure investments. In Egypt, the cost of an infrastructure job is as low as US$2,621 in the roads and bridge construction sector, but more than four times higher in the electricity-generating sector, and nearly seven times higher in the transport and communications sector. Sectors also differ in their propensity to generate indirect jobs. It depends on the extent to which the sector requires inputs from other sectors to produce its output. Based on the Egyptian data, the ratio of all jobs to the number of direct jobs was as low as 1.09 for construction in roads and bridges, whereas it was 1.82 for transport and communications.

Implications of Using Labor-Intensive Technologies in the Maintenance of Unpaved Roads

Often the need to save resources and achieve different policy goals affects the choice between labor- and capital-intensive technologies in infrastructure. Clearly, the former is more likely to increase the total amount of employment generated, and it may also reduce overall costs. This possibility is discussed in this section in the context of unpaved roads maintenance.

Labor-intensive approaches to road maintenance can be a good choice in countries where job creation is a priority. In addition to the positive impact on employment creation, labor-intensive technologies can lead to cost savings relative to equipment-intensive alternatives. Devereux and Solomon (2006) reported that some labor-intensive programs have provided up to 30 percent cost savings, and others have identified even up to 50 percent savings.

However, focusing only on reducing the overall investment amount is probably not the best criterion when considering labor-intensive technologies. The cost structure of labor-intensive infrastructure provision is different from the equipment-intensive alternative as the former includes components like training and development of institutional capacity. Direct comparisons of labor versus nonlabor costs can therefore be misleading.

In this study, we assume that labor-intensive technologies for unpaved roads can realize up to 30 percent in cost savings without hurting quality (see results discussed by Del Ninno, Subbarao, and Milazzo 2009; Devereux and Solomon 2006). This implies that unit costs and depreciation rates are lower under the labor-intensive technology alternative than the capital-intensive one (table 3.14). The use of labor-intensive technologies reduces investment needs in the region on average by 0.3 percent of GDP. With the switch from equipment-intensive to labor-intensive type of technology, annual investment needs decrease the most in the GCC and the OECs (about US$2 billion per year), whereas they have a smaller impact in the OICs (see table 3.15).

Table 3.14   Road Maintenance and Rehabilitation Program by Type of Technology
U.S. dollars

	Equipment-intensive technology	Labor-intensive technology
Unit costs		
Routine	2,000	1,400
Periodic	10,000	7,000
Rehabilitation	15,000	10,500
Maintenance and rehabilitation annual cost per km	3,650	2,555
Unit costs for new roads	50,000	50,000
Depreciation rate (%)	7.2	5.1

Source: World Bank data.
Note: km = Kilometers.

Table 3.15   Investment Needs for Unpaved Road Maintenance by Type of Technology

Technology	OIC	OEC	GCC	MENA
% of GDP				
Labor intensive	0.5	1.7	1.0	1.1
Equipment intensive	0.6	2.1	1.3	1.4
Difference	0.1	0.4	0.3	0.3
US$ million				
Labor intensive	1,764	7,541	7,429	16,734
Equipment intensive	2,246	9,497	9,461	21,204
Difference	482	1,956	2,032	4,470

Source: World Bank data.
Note: GCC = Gulf Cooperation Council; GDP = gross domestic product; MENA = Middle East and North Africa;
OEC = developing oil exporting country; OIC = oil importing country.

Annex 3A Constructing Hybrid Estimates of Employment Linked to Investment

The standard IO model of an economy links the gross output of a sector to the final demand for that sector and the intermediate demands made by other sectors for its output, as follows:

$$X = A\,X + F, \tag{3A.1}$$

where X is a vector of gross outputs of the N sectors of the economy; F is a vector of final demands for these sectors; and A is the $N \times N$ matrix of technical coefficients that indicate how much output from sector i is directly required to produce one unit of sector j. Gross output is measured in current money terms, as defined in the IO table.

The gross output is then related to final demand by equation 3A.2, where the coefficient matrix B measures the total amount of sector i that is required to be produced to satisfy the direct and indirect demands produced by one unit increase in the final demand for sector j:

$$X = (I - A)^{-1}\,F \equiv B\,F. \tag{3A.2}$$

To convert output figures into employment figures, a vector of employment levels per unit of output is required (usually measured in full-time equivalent employment units) represented by w. The direct employment effect of one unit increase in final demand for sector j would be denoted by w_j, and the average cost per direct job would be given by the inverse of w_j. The values of employment per unit of output can be derived by dividing the share of the compensation paid to employees by the wage plus benefit level of a full-time employee.

Hence, one unit increase in the demand for sector j will generate direct plus indirect employment, as expressed in equation 3A.3:

$$E_j = \sum_i w_i \, B_{ij}. \tag{3A.3}$$

The type I multiplier $M(I)_j$ for sector j is then defined by equation 3A.4:

$$M(I)_j = \sum_i w_i \, B_{ij} / w_j. \tag{3A.4}$$

To allow for induced effects from consumption generated by extra incomes from direct and indirect effects, the IO matrix is expanded to incorporate a vector of household expenditures on each sector when income increases by one unit. The calculation of the extended B matrix is then linked to the augmented A matrix, and the calculation of the type II multiplier proceeds analogously using the extended B matrix.

The employment and multiplier calculations are initially based on the year of the IO table. It is assumed that over time, all sector wages (used to calculate the sector employment coefficients) increase with productivity and inflation by the same rate as nominal GDP per capita. Denoting this value by $g(0)$ for the year of the IO table, and by $g(1)$ for the year required, the employment generated by one unit increase in gross output is given by equation 3A.5:

$$E_j(1) = \sum_i w_i \left(\frac{g(0)}{g(1)} \right) B_{ij}. \tag{3A.5}$$

As GDP per capita increases, the direct plus indirect employment generated by a given expenditure declines. The type I multiplier is unaffected by the rise in GDP per capita because the scaling factors enter both the numerator and the denominator. The cost per job is obtained by dividing the size of the unit expenditure by the employment created according to equation 3A.5 (for direct plus indirect jobs), and this indicates that costs per job will rise as $g(1)$ increases relative to $g(0)$.

A similar correction is required for comparisons across economies because, even if it can be assumed that the physical IO matrices are similar, the wage rates would be different reflecting general labor productivity differences. Equation 3A.5 can be interpreted as providing an estimate of employment generated in country $C(1)$ based on an actual IO table from country $C(0)$. If GDP per capita is higher in country $C(1)$ than in country

C(0), the amount of employment generated by the same expenditure would be lower in C(1) than in C(0), and the cost per job would be higher.

In cases where there is disaggregate employee compensation by skill levels, and wage rates for the different skill groups, it is possible to estimate employment generated by skill group in response to investment spending in a sector. For the case of two skill levels, the employment levels generated in the base year in sector j by a unit increase in demand can be denoted $w\alpha_i$ and $w\beta_i$. The total number of direct and indirect skill level α jobs created will be:

$$E\alpha_j = \sum_i w\alpha_i B_{ij}. \qquad (3A.6)$$

To estimate the number of skill level α jobs that would be created in year 1, equation 3A.6 is modified following equation 3A.5. That is, all labor costs are assumed to increase at the rate of growth of nominal GDP per capita:

$$E\alpha_j(1) = \sum_i w\alpha_i \left(\frac{g(0)}{g(1)} \right) B_{ij}. \qquad (3A.7)$$

The following example illustrates the adjustments discussed in this annex. In the case of the Egyptian IO table, data are given on total employee compensation and jobs created. The latter are calculated based on the basic wage. To the extent that the total payment to employees is above the basic wage, the calculation based on basic wages would result in an overestimation of the number of jobs created, whereas the correct estimate is assumed to be 85 percent of the number shown by ILO (2010).

In the year for which the Egyptian IO table was made, the average cost of one type II job created by investment spending in the water and sewage sector in Egypt was LE 27,359. By 2009, it was estimated that the cost of a job would have risen to LE 32,680 (US$6,096), reflecting the increase in per capita GDP.

The cost of creating one direct job is higher than the cost of creating one type II job, as direct job creation does not factor in the knock-on effects of investment on indirect and induced employment. It is also important to recognize that the cost of one direct job as calculated from an IO table is substantially higher than the employee compensation paid to a single worker. Additional costs are incurred for buying inputs from other sectors, leakages through imports, taxes on production, and the operating surplus of companies. In the case discussed in box 3A.1, direct labor costs accounted for about 15 percent of total spending.

Box 3A.1

Calculation of the Cost of a Type II Job Using a Hybrid Approach

The IO table for Egypt for 2007/08 provided information for the water and sewage sector based on incremental sector expenditure of 1,000 Egyptian pounds (LE):

(1)	Direct employee compensation[a]	= LE 147
(2)	Direct + indirect employee compensation[a]	= LE 192
(3)	Direct + indirect + induced employee compensation[a]	= LE 243
(4)	Sector average annual basic wage[a]	= LE 4,141
(5)	Sector average annual total wage	= (4)/0.85 = LE 4,872
(6)	Direct jobs via basic wage[a]	= 0.036 FTE
(7)	Direct + indirect jobs via basic wage[a]	= 0.039 FTE
(8)	Direct + indirect + induced jobs via basic wage[a]	= 0.043 FTE
(9)	Type I multiplier[a]	= (7)/(6) = 1.08
(10)	Type II multiplier[a]	= (8)/(6) = 1.21
(11)	GDP per capita in current LE in 2007/08	= 10,144
(12)	GDP per capita in current LE in 2009	= 12,531
(13)	Cost of one job (type II) in 2007/08	= 1,000/(8)/0.85 = LE 27,359
(14)	Cost of one direct job in 2007/08	= 1,000/(6)/0.85 = LE 32,680
(15)	Estimated cost of one job (type II) in 2009	= (12) × (13)/(11) = 33,797 LE
(16)	Exchange rate to US$ in 2009	= 5.544
(17)	GDP per capita in current US$ in 2009	= 2,270
(18)	Estimated cost of one job (type II) in current US$ in 2009	= (15)/(16) = 6,096

To illustrate the use of Egyptian data for extrapolation to another country, the cases of Djibouti and Jordan are illustrated for type II jobs in the water and sewage sector.

(19)	GDP per capita in current US$ in 2009 in Djibouti	= 1,214
(20)	GDP per capita in current US$ in 2009 in Jordan	= 4,212
(21)	Estimated cost of one type II job in Djibouti in current US$ in 2009	= (19) × (18)/(17) = 3,260
(22)	Estimated cost of one type II job in Jordan in current US$ in 2009	= (20) × (18)/(17) = 11,311

Sources: ILO 2010; World Bank data.
Note: FTE = full-time equivalents; GDP = gross domestic product.
a. Indicates data taken from IO table.

Based on the estimated cost of generating one type II job in Egypt in 2009, and allowing for the difference in GDP per capita, the estimated cost of a type II job created by investment in the water and sewage sector in Djibouti in 2009 is US$3,260 and US$11,311 in Jordan. This method can be extended to all sectors for which there is information in the Egyptian IO table. The variation in wages in the sector, as indexed by GDP per capita, result in large differences in the costs of job creation between Djibouti and Jordan, reflecting the more than threefold difference in GDP per capita.

Annex 3B Estimated Shares of Inputs in Different Types of Infrastructure

Type of Infrastructure	Qualified workers	Nonqualified workers	Domestic material inputs	Imported inputs	Other inputs
Paved roads	0.15	0.06	0.49	0.16	0.14
Roads*	0.03	0.09	0.22	0.63	0.03
Rail lines**	0.13	0.01	0.52	0.24	0.10
Ports	0.10	0.10	0.80	0.00	0.00
Telephone mainlines	0.15	0.15	0.30	0.24	0.16
Mobile lines***	0.15	0.15	0.30	0.24	0.16
Electricity generation	0.10	0.00	0.90	0.00	0.00
Electricity access	0.14	0.07	0.26	0.53	0.00
Water	0.25	0.25	0.40	0.10	0.00
Sanitation	0.08	0.56	0.32	0.04	0.00

Sources: Schwartz, Andres, and Dragoiu 2009; World Bank data.
Notes: *The ratio for job creation in rail versus road in the US was adapted to the estimates of LAC.
**The percentages for railways were adapted from Heintz, Pollin, and Garrett-Peltier (2009).
***The estimates for telecommunication were adapted from Foreman and Beauvais (1999). They found the capital/network, sales and marketing, and other input shares in the mobile phone industry to be on average 0.273, 0.408, and 0.319, respectively. We adapted these numbers to provide an approximation of the actual share of labor inputs.

Annex 3C Potential for Job Creation in the Three Groups of MENA Countries

Sector	Direct jobs/US$ billion, in the sector	Share of investment (percent)	Direct job/US$ billion, in infrastructure	Total jobs (weighted)
GCC countries				
Paved roads	47,500	12.00	3,800	4,141
Roads	22,500	28.00	4,200	4,577

(continued next page)

Annex 3C *(continued)*

Sector	Direct jobs/US$ billion, in the sector	Share of investment (percent)	Direct job/US$ billion, in infrastructure	Total jobs (weighted)
Rail lines	83,333	0.00	0	0
Ports	41,667	4.00	1,111	1,789
Telephone mainlines	104,167	0.80	333	447
Mobile lines	104,167	3.60	1,500	2,010
Electricity generation	25,000	48.40	8,067	10,891
Electricity access	46,667	1.20	373	556
Water	104,167	0.60	417	504
Sanitation	113,333	1.40	1,058	1,280
Total	n.a.	100.00	20,859	26,195
OICs				
Paved roads	95,000	23.53	22,353	24,359
Roads	45,000	10.08	4,538	4,945
Rail lines	166,667	1.68	1,148	2,090
Ports	83,333	1.68	1,401	2,255
Telephone mainlines	208,333	3.03	3,782	5,067
Mobile lines	208,333	9.92	12,395	16,609
Electricity generation	50,000	35.29	17,647	23,826
Electricity access	93,333	7.23	6,745	10,050
Water	208,333	3.19	6,653	8,050
Sanitation	226,667	4.37	9,905	11,985
Total	n.a.	100.00	86,567	109,236
OECs				
Paved roads	95.000	25.16	11,952	13,025
Roads	45.000	19.57	4,404	4,799
Rail lines	166.667	0.93	318	579
Ports	83.333	0.00	0	0
Telephone mainlines	208.333	3.08	1,922	2,576
Mobile lines	208.333	6.90	4,310	5,776
Electricity generation	50.000	34.58	8,644	11,670
Electricity access	93.333	4.47	2,088	3,110
Water	208.333	2.24	2,330	2,819
Sanitation	226.667	3.08	3,486	4,218
Total	n.a.	100.00	39,454	48,572

Sources: Bacon and Kojima 2011; Foreman and Beauvais 1999; Gardiner and Theobald 2009; ILO 2011; Schwartz, Andres, and Dragoiu 2009; Tong 2010; World Bank data.

Note: GCC = Gulf Cooperation Council; OEC = developing oil exporting country; OIC = oil importing country; n.a.= not applicable.

Notes

1. In some cases this number is available, so there is no need to do the estimation.

2. In some countries, a fine level of disaggregation is used so that a sector can easily be identified as being representative of a particular planned future expenditure. In cases where a coarser level of disaggregation is used, the multiplier is less accurate.

3. The type II multiplier is the ratio of all jobs created to the number of direct jobs.

4. Schwartz, Andres, and Dragoiu (2009) showed that wages in the construction sector in South America varied between US$1.39 and US$4.28 an hour, but based their calculations on an average wage rate net of benefits of US$2.55 an hour across the region.

5. Data for Qatar and the United Arab Emirates were omitted, as they are extreme outliers with very high GDP per capita and low construction wages.

6. See IO tables used in Bekhet (2011) for the case of Malaysia and Tregenna (2007) for the case of South Africa.

7. IO tables are available for a number of countries in the MENA region, but only the IO table for Egypt has been prepared in a form that provides employment data.

8. Annex 3A discusses the hybrid method of estimating employment and illustrates the method of estimating the cost of type II employment creation in Djibouti and Jordan, using data from Egypt's IO table.

9. Lack of current GDP data for the West Bank and Gaza precluded the use of the hybrid method in that case.

10. It is important to note that the estimate for this sector includes all activities, not just the construction activities within the transport and communications sector.

11. Since the same sector weights are applied to each country, the total number of jobs created is proportional to GDP per capita—the scaling factor applied to every sector within a country.

12. The regional average is a weighted average with weights corresponding to countries' population numbers in 2009.

13. Schwartz, Andres, and Dragoiu (2009) assume hourly wages gross of benefits to be respectively US$6 and US$3 for qualified and nonqualified workers in LAC.

14. The data in Gardiner and Theobald (2007) for Latin America are consistent with the ones used in Schwartz, Andres, and Dragoiu (2009), allowing us to use a similar methodology.

15. Converting to US$ for the hourly wage, the median wage in construction is approximately US$3.70.

16. The percentages for railways were adapted from Heintz, Pollin, and Garrett-Peltier (2009). The ratio of job creation in rail versus road in the United States was adapted to the estimates of LAC. The estimates for telecommunication were adapted from Foreman and Beauvais (1999). They found the capital/network, sales and marketing, and other input shares in the mobile phone industry to be on average 0.273, 0.408, and 0.319, respectively. We adapted these figures to provide an approximation of the actual share of labor inputs. The estimated input shares are given in annex 3B.

17. The multiplier of 4 means there is one indirect job per one direct job and one induced job per one direct and one indirect job.

18. Sectoral results are presented in annex 3C.

References

Babcock, M., J. Leatherman, M. Melichar, and E. Landman. 2010. "*Economic Impacts of the Kansas Comprehensive Transportation Program (CTP) Highway Construction and Maintenance Activities.*" Report No. K-TRAN:KSU-10-4, Kansas State University Transportation Center, Manhattan, Kansas. http://transport.ksu.edu/files/transport/imported/Reports/2010/KSU104_FinalRep.pdf

Bacon, R. and M. Kojima. 2011. *Issues in Estimating the Employment Generated by Energy Sector Activities.* Sustainable Energy Department, World Bank, Washington, DC. http://siteresources.worldbank.org/EXTENERGY2/Resources/MeasuringEmploymentImpactofEnergySector.pdf.

Bekhet, H. 2011. "Output, Income and Employment Multipliers in Malaysian Economy: Input-Output Approach." *International Business Research* 4 (1): 208–23.

CH2MHILL. 2009. *Economic Impact Analysis for the Teanaway Solar Reserve, Kittitas County, Washington.* http://teanawaysolarreserve.com/wp-content/uploads/2010/05/Teanaway_Economic_Impact_Analysis_10_07_09.pdf.

Del Ninno, C., K. Subbarao, and A. Milazzo. 2009. "How to Make Public Works Work: A Review of the Experiences." SP Discussion Paper No. 0905, Social Protection and Labor, World Bank, Washington, DC.

Devereux, S., and C. Solomon. 2006. "Employment Creation Programmes: The International Experience." Issues in Employment and Poverty Discussion Paper 24, Economic and Labour Market Analysis Department, International Labour Organization, Geneva.

DIT (Indian Department of Information Technology). 2007. *E-Readiness Assessment Report 2005.* New Delhi: DIT. http://www.ncaer.org/Downloads/Reports/E-Readiness2005.pdf.

Foreman, R., and E. Beauvais. 1999. "Scale Economies in Cellular Telephony: Size Matters." *Journal of Regulatory Economics* 16: 297–306.

Gardiner & Theobald. 2009. *International Construction Cost Survey*. London: Gardiner & Theobald. http://www.gardiner.com/assets/files/files/f8d864e655 dff0adcb60ac1ba0f0cdb0c4a60b04/2008%20International% 20Construction%20Cost%20US%20$%20Version.pdf.

Heintz, J., R. Pollin, and H. Garrett-Peltier. 2009. *How Infrastructure Investments Support the U.S. Economy: Employment, Productivity, and Growth*. Amherst, MA: Political Economy Research Institute, University of Massachusetts.

ILO (International Labour Organization). 2010. *Measuring the Impact of the Egyptian Fiscal Stimulus Package 2008/2009*. Cairo: ILO.

———. 2011. *Global Employment Trends 2011*. Geneva: ILO.

Ishihara, S., and C. Bennett. 2010. "Improving Local Roads and Creating Jobs Through Rapid Response Projects: Lessons from Armenia Lifeline Roads Improvement Project." Roads and Highways Thematic Group, Transport Notes: TRN-39, World Bank, Washington, DC.

LECG (Law and Economics Consulting Group). 2009. *The Economic Benefits from Investment in Advanced Mobile Infrastructure and Services: the Case of Thailand*. London: LECG. http://www.gsmamobilebroadband .com/upload/resources/files/LECG_Thailand_report_Final_Oct09.pdf.

Pfeifenberger, J., J. Chang, D. Hou, and K. Madjarov. 2010. *Job and Economic Benefits of Transmission and Wind Generation Investments in the SPP Region*. Cambridge, MA: The Brattle Group. http://www.brattle.com/_documents /UploadLibrary/Upload859.pdf.

REPP (Renewable Energy Policy Project). 2001. *The Work That Goes into Renewable Energy*. Research Report 13, REPP, Washington, DC. http://www .repp.org/articles/static/1/binaries/LABOR_FINAL_REV.pdf.

Schwartz, J., L. Andres, and G. Dragoiu. 2009. "Crisis in Latin America: Infrastructure Investment, Employment, and the Expectations of Stimulus." Policy Research Working Paper 5009, World Bank, Washington, DC.

Scottish Government. 2011. "Input-output-introduction." Scottish Government, http://www.scotland.gov.uk/Topics/Statistics/Browse/Economy/Input-Output.

Tong, Q. 2010. "Wage Structure in the United Arab Emirates." Institute for Social and Economic Research. Working Paper, Zayed University, Abu Dhabi.

Tregenna, F. 2007. *The Contribution of Manufacturing and Services Sectors to Growth and Employment in South Africa*. Pretoria, HSRC.

Vesin, V. 2011. "Transport and Employment." MENA Working Note, World Bank, Washington, DC.

World Bank. 2010. "Bangladesh—Rural Transport Improvement Project, Implementation Status Results Report." World Bank, Washington, DC.

CHAPTER 4

Long-Term Employment Effects through the Growth Channel

This chapter investigates the contribution of infrastructure investments to growth, and thus job creation. The idea about this contribution is based on the two-pronged hypothesis that improved infrastructure leads to economic growth and that economic growth leads to increased employment. Quantifying this hypothesis requires first of all an understanding of the extent to which infrastructure impacts growth. In a recent meta-analysis of over 100 studies, Estache and Garsous (2011) found that the effect depends on three main factors: (1) the specific indicators used to approximate infrastructure[1], (2) the time period analyzed[2], and (3) the level of development of the country in question.[3] Taking these characteristics into account facilitates the generation of a relatively robust estimate of the average elasticity of growth to infrastructure, which can be used to estimate the average growth impact of various levels of infrastructure investment on growth in the Middle East and North Africa (MENA). Second, one needs to assess the impact of economic growth on job creation, given by the elasticity of employment to growth. The elasticity of employment to infrastructure can then be derived from the elasticity of growth to infrastructure and the elasticity of employment to infrastructure.

Output Elasticity with Respect to Infrastructure

With Y_t as the economic output at time t—measured by the gross domestic product (GDP) of a country—and Inf_t as the stock of infrastructure at time t, the basic definition for the output growth elasticity with respect to infrastructure (Inf) is given by the following:

$$\varepsilon_{Inf} = \frac{(Y_t - Y_{t-1})/Y_{t-1}}{(Inf_t - Inf_{t-1})/Inf_{t-1}}. \tag{4.1}$$

This elasticity measures the percentage point increase in output, given a percentage point increase in the stock of infrastructure. The elasticity can be estimated using historical data and used to get a sense of the infrastructure investment needs under various growth scenarios. Alternatively, one can use it to assess the extent to which infrastructure commitments considered by governments will lead to growth.

Since there are no specific growth elasticities with respect to infrastructure for the MENA region or countries, it is necessary to rely on a survey of international experience in developing countries to obtain an estimate of the output elasticity with respect to infrastructure. Although there is quite a large literature on the topic, relatively few studies cover developing countries. The basic average elasticity used for the MENA sample, and an associated confidence interval, draw on the estimation results from 10 studies focusing on developing countries presented in table 4.1. These are relatively high elasticities when compared to those used for developed countries—a fact consistent with one of the lessons of the meta-analysis quoted earlier. However, the variance is large enough to be concerned about the reliability of the average elasticity derived from this sample.

To assess the robustness of the elasticity, we built a confidence interval for the mean μ of this sample. The empirical mean and the standard error of this sample are given by $\bar{x} = 0.22$ and $s = 0.17$, respectively. Therefore, assuming normality, we have in the following:

$$p\left(-1.96 \leq \frac{0.22 - \mu}{\frac{0.17}{\sqrt{n-1}}} \leq 1.96\right) = 0.95. \tag{4.2}$$

Consequently, there is only a 5 percent chance that μ does not fall into the following interval:

$$0.115 \leq \mu \leq 0.325. \tag{4.3}$$

Table 4.1   Studies Providing Estimates of the Output Elasticity with Respect to Infrastructure

Authors	Estimated Elasticity
Dessus and Herrera 2000	0.13
Gwartney, Helcombe, and Lawson 2006	0.17
Khan and Kumar 1997 (Africa)	0.32
Khan and Kumar 1997 (Asia)	0.26
Nazmi and Ramirez 1997	0.13
Odedokun 1997	0.03
Ram 1986	0.37
Ram 1996	0.30
Ramirez 1998	0.58
Sánchez-Robles 1998	0.00
Sridhar and Sridhar 2004	0.10

The boundaries of this interval define reasonably robust lower and upper bounds for the output elasticity with respect to infrastructure in developing countries. These bounds will be used in this report to compensate for the lack of a region-specific estimate.

Employment Elasticity with Respect to Economic Output

The employment elasticity with respect to economic output (GDP) growth E_t is defined as the percentage change in the aggregate level of employment in the economy given a percentage point increase in economic output at time t:

$$\varepsilon_E = \frac{(E_t - E_{t-1})/E_{t-1}}{(Y_t - Y_{t-1})/Y_{t-1}}. \tag{4.4}$$

This elasticity can be used to get a sense of how much job creation could be expected to result from various growth scenarios. In contrast to the growth elasticity with respect to infrastructure, there is no need to extrapolate the values of this elasticity from international estimates as estimation for the region and countries can be derived using International Labour Organization (ILO) data.

The elasticities presented in table 4.2 show that some countries' employment levels are particularly sensitive to growth, indicating that they could also be more receptive to policy efforts to promote job creation in the short run. Table 4.2 also shows aggregate elasticities for the

Table 4.2   Employment Elasticities with Respect to GDP in MENA, 2009

Country/region	Elasticity
Gulf Cooperation Council (GCC)	
Bahrain	0.44
Kuwait	0.41
Oman	0.50
Qatar	1.26
Saudi Arabia	1.00
United Arab Emirates	0.88
Average	*0.89*
Developing oil exporting countries (OECs)	
Algeria	1.29
Iran, Islamic Rep.	0.59
Iraq	0.49
Libya	0.49
Syrian Arab Republic	0.65
Yemen, Rep.	1.12
Average	*0.78*
Oil importing countries (OICs)	
Egypt, Arab Rep.	0.82
Jordan	0.69
Lebanon	0.52
Morocco	0.50
Tunisia	0.55
Average	*0.69*
MENA	0.77
Middle East	0.71
North Africa	0.84

Source: International Labour Organization (ILO) (key indicators of the labor market).
Note: MENA = Middle East and North Africa.

region and subregions. These were computed as a weighted average of the country-specific elasticities, with weights reflecting the share of a country's employment in the total regional employment. Although countries are commonly grouped into regional and subregional aggregates, the heterogeneity of country-specific elasticities suggests that the practice of grouping countries might lead to loss of important information. The only group with some comparability is the one encompassing the OICs as they all have elasticities below 1.

Employment Elasticity with Respect to Infrastructure

The easiest approximation of the employment elasticity with respect to infrastructure ε can be obtained from the following expression, which combines the employment-growth elasticity and the growth-infrastructure elasticity:

$$\varepsilon = \frac{(E_t - E_{t-1})/E_{t-1}}{(Y_t - Y_{t-1})/Y_{t-1}} \times \frac{(Y_t - Y_{t-1})/Y_{t-1}}{(\text{Inf}_t - \text{Inf}_{t-1})/\text{Inf}_{t-1}}. \tag{4.5}$$

The lower and upper bounds for the employment elasticity with respect to infrastructure can hence be calculated using the latest figures for employment-growth elasticity and the lower and upper bounds of the output elasticity with respect to infrastructure. Table 4.3 presents

Table 4.3   Lower and Upper Bounds for the Employment Elasticity with Respect to Infrastructure

Country/region	Lower	Upper
GCC		
Bahrain	0.05	0.14
Kuwait	0.05	0.13
Oman	0.06	0.16
Qatar	0.14	0.41
Saudi Arabia	0.12	0.33
United Arab Emirates	0.10	0.29
Average	0.10	0.29
OECs		
Algeria	0.15	0.42
Iran, Islamic Rep.	0.07	0.19
Iraq	0.06	0.16
Libya	0.06	0.16
Syrian Arab Republic	0.07	0.21
Yemen, Rep.	0.13	0.36
Average	0.09	0.25
OICs		
Egypt, Arab Rep.	0.09	0.26
Jordan	0.08	0.22
Lebanon	0.06	0.17
Morocco	0.06	0.16
Tunisia	0.06	0.18
Average	0.08	0.23
Middle East	0.08	0.23
North Africa	0.10	0.27
MENA	0.09	0.25

Source: Based on ILO data.
Note: GCC = Gulf Cooperation Council; MENA = Middle East and North Africa; OEC = developing oil exporting country; OIC = oil importing country.

lower and upper bounds of the employment elasticity with respect to infrastructure at the regional and country levels. The information contained in table 4.3 implies that a 1 percent increase in the infrastructure capital stock would increase employment in the MENA region by between 0.10 and 0.25 percent. The employment growth elasticities and these bounds form the foundation on which simulations on the impact of infrastructure expansion on jobs in the region can be undertaken.

Long-Run Employment Response to Infrastructure Investment

This section estimates the employment response induced by infrastructure investment resulting in 1 percentage point additional growth using equation 4.4. The wide range of employment-infrastructure elasticities presented in table 4.3 implies that the infrastructure investment required to boost growth by a percentage point would vary by country. The lower the growth elasticity with respect to infrastructure, the higher the required increase in the stock of infrastructure. For example, the lower bound of the elasticity suggests that an increase of 8.7 percent in the stock of infrastructure is required to add a percentage point to growth in the MENA region. This is the more likely scenario in high-income MENA, comprising the GCC economies and some upper middle-income MENA countries, as in the more developed countries the likely growth impact of an additional unit of infrastructure investment tends to be smaller. In the case of the upper bound elasticity, the required increase in the infrastructure stock is just 3.1 percent. However, the estimated employment response to growth of 1 percent depends only on the employment growth elasticity and the level of employment in 2009. Thus, we get one set of estimates by subgroup and these are shown in table 4.4.

The results suggest that the employment response induced by infrastructure investment, resulting in an additional growth of 1 percentage point, is expected to lead to a total of slightly more than 9 million additional jobs in the course of 10 years in MENA, or a little less than 1 million jobs per year. Half of these jobs are expected to be located in the Middle East and the other half in North Africa. This response is significant and accounts for approximately 30 percent of the jobs created during the 2000s. Had these jobs been created during the 2000s, the unemployment rate would be substantially lower than the 10 percent registered at the end of the 2000s. Technological choice (i.e., a switch to labor-intensive technologies) could enhance the employment creation

Table 4.4   Employment Response to Infrastructure Investment Resulting in a Percentage Point Additional Growth
millions, over a decade

Country/region	Number of jobs
GCC	1.4
OEC	4.7
OIC	2.9
Middle East	4.5
North Africa	4.5
MENA	9.0

Source: Based on 2009 employment levels from International Labour Organization (ILO).
Note: GCC = Gulf Cooperation Council; MENA = Middle East and North Africa; OEC = developing oil exporting country; OIC = oil importing country.

effect of infrastructure investment. Other factors may also make a difference, such as increased labor mobility, improved procurement rules, and training and transition subsidies. These estimates depend on the magnitude of the employment-growth elasticities in table 4.2. The lower these elasticities, the lower will be the growth response of additional growth in response to infrastructure investment.

Notes

1. Using energy as a proxy guarantees a much stronger impact than using water or even telecoms, and a synthetic indicator provides an intermediate level of impact as expected.

2. The impact was stronger in the 1950s and 1960s than in the last two decades.

3. The less developed the country, the higher the likely impact. However, this result is not as statistically robust as expected.

References

Dessus, S., and R. Herrera. 2000. "Public Capital and Growth Revisited: A Panel Data Assessment." *Economic Development and Cultural Change* 48: 407–18.

Estache, A., and G. Garsous. 2011. "Drivers of the Impact of Infrastructure on Growth: A Meta-Analysis." ECARES working paper, Université Libre de Bruxelles, Brussels.

Gwartney, J., R. Holcombe, and R. Lawson. 2006. "Institutions and the Impact of Investment on Growth." *Kyklos* 59 (2): 255–73.

Khan, M., and M. Kumar. 1997. "Public and Private Investment and the Growth Process in Developing Countries." *Logistics and Transportation Review* 59 (1): 69–88.

Nazmi, N., and M. Ramirez. 1997. "Public and Private Investment and Economic Growth in Mexico." *Contemporary Economic Policy* 15 (1): 65–75.

Odedokun, M. 1997. "Relative Effects of Public versus Private Investment Spending on Economic Efficiency and Growth in Developing Countries." *Applied Economics* 29 (10): 1325–36.

Ram, R. 1986. "Government Size and Economic Growth: A New Framework and Some Evidence from Cross-Section and Time-Series Data." *American Economic Review* 76: 191–203.

———. 1996. "Productivity of Public Capital and Private Investment in Developing Countries: A Broad International Perspective." *World Development* 24: 1373–78.

Ramirez, M. 1998. "Does Public Investment Enhance Productivity Growth in Mexico? A Cointegration Analysis." *Eastern Economic Journal* 24 (1): 63–82.

Sánchez-Robles, B. 1998. "Infrastructure Investment and Growth: Some Empirical Evidence." *Contemporary Economic Policy* 16 (1): 98–109.

Sridhar, K., and V. Sridhar. 2004. "Telecommunications, Infrastructure and Economic Growth: Evidence from Developing Countries." Working Paper 14, National Institute of Public Finance and Policy, New Delhi.

CHAPTER 5

Policy Implications

Infrastructure investment has the potential to create jobs in a short span of time, while providing a foundation for future growth. This is especially important in the oil importing countries (OICs), where the infrastructure gap is the greatest and employment needs are growing. However, it is also likely to be most difficult in these countries because of strained finances. Going forward, government decisions on the types of spending to expand and what to downsize in order to achieve balanced budgets will have important implications for jobs.

Not all jobs are equal, so investments in infrastructure will need to be prioritized based on the employment and infrastructure needs of the country. For example, road and bridge construction projects will have a direct impact on creation of relatively low-skilled jobs. These types of projects will be especially effective in addressing job-related concerns in countries where there is a large pool of relatively unskilled and unemployed people. This is the case in many developing countries in the Middle East and North Africa (MENA), where the majority of the unemployed do not have tertiary education. By contrast, projects in transport and communication services have large indirect effects and, therefore, the ability to create a diverse set of jobs for workers with different skill levels. These projects will appeal to policy makers in countries where the unemployed have the ability to acquire specialized skills relatively quickly.

This chapter discusses the impact of short-term support for employment creation through infrastructure spending on long-term employment and complementary policies needed to ensure beneficial outcomes. Public works and different types of subsidized employment programs have been used widely to make it easier for people who cannot find unsubsidized jobs to find employment and acquire on-the-job skills. These programs are necessary, for instance, to address structural issues, which will not be addressed through market forces alone as economies grow bigger. Subsidized employment programs in infrastructure and construction have typically been used to create employment opportunities for low-skilled workers.

The first section of this chapter reviews evidence on the effect of wage subsidies on the long-term employability of workers and suggests that training plays an important role in boosting job creation in the long run. The second section analyzes the types of effective training. The third section offers ways to bring down training costs by effective targeting, whereas section four looks at the broader question of whether it is actually desirable to subsidize job creation in the long run. The final section discusses the fiscal costs and benefits of job creation programs. Prudent planning of infrastructure development and execution of infrastructure projects will be critical for growth and job creation, as poor governance and weak institutions are the greatest risks in using infrastructure as a strategy to enhance employment and growth in MENA countries.

Subsidized Employment Programs and Job Creation

Boosting short-term job creation in developing MENA economies is desirable, particularly in the context of recent political developments. Subsidized employment programs should be designed to ensure that there is a positive spillover to long-run employment and employability. The literature suggests that it is possible and relatively easy—although potentially costly—to start up or catalyze long-term job creation. Subsidized jobs help beneficiaries become employed, facilitating their future employment (Bell and Orr 1994; Richardson 1998). Such an effect, however, requires competences obtained during employment in the infrastructure sector to be transferable to jobs in other sectors. Many researchers also point to risks of downward pressure on wages. Such risks could result from a potential increase in the supply of qualified workers with experience in the infrastructure sector. As infrastructure jobs represent only 15–25 percent of total jobs, the risk of wage pressures may not be vast but cannot be ignored.

Subsidized employment programs tend to enhance short-term job creation but have no impact on future employability (McCord and van Seventer 2004; Richardson 1998). This is because of (1) stigmatization—having a subsidized job is a signal of not being able to get a "real" job, and this can be used by firms as a screening device (Burtless 1985)—and (2) disqualification—the beneficiaries are often asked to take unskilled jobs that do not enhance their employability. For instance, Boeri (1997) has found that participation in public works schemes can reduce the chance of finding a regular job.

Research suggests that one way of offsetting any negative impact of subsidized employment programs is to ensure proper training of subsidized workers. When combined with training and counseling, subsidized programs significantly increase future employability (Katz 1996; Martin and Grubb 2001). The longer the duration of employment under the subsidized programs, the higher is the probability of future inclusion in the "normal" labor market (Gagliarducci 2005). The training provided as part of the subsidized job addresses underprovision of training by private firms when the corresponding human capital is transferable.

During the early 1990s, the World Bank conducted research on this topic, as summarized in Rama (2003). One World Bank project concerning railways in Brazil provided a unique experience in the creation and design of training programs, aimed at minimizing the time spent unemployed and maximizing the workers' chances of finding a job outside of infrastructure (Estache, Schmitt, and Sydenstricker 2000). The project included financing for training of workers who had lost their jobs as a result of privatization programs and also provided experience in building national capacity to run decentralized training centers, and in some instances, the outsourcing of training. The project also provided an ex-post evaluation of the design of incentives given to workers to enroll for the training programs.

Types of Training for Lasting Job Creation

Experience shows that the design of training should be given as much attention as the design of subsidized employment programs. Research suggests that if there is a role for subsidies, in particular in long-term programs, those subsidies should be focused on sectors where the market alone fails to provide sufficient employment, in other words, where there is a mismatch between the supply and demand for skills. As many workers are unskilled, the challenge is to identify the various types of training required.

Ideally, training should start with a general orientation aimed at providing a basis on which more specialized training can be done as needed. In theory, workers are more likely to acquire general training when markets are competitive and the turnover is high (Wasmer 2006). However, subsidized jobs for low-skilled workers may reduce incentives to become skilled—an effect amplified by the fact that taxes used to pay for subsidies may result in an additional tax burden for skilled workers (Oskamp and Snower 2006). Also, there is no reason to provide training specific to the infrastructure sector if the subsidized job is temporary and the objective of the training is to facilitate inclusion into the general labor market rather than the infrastructure sector.

Specialized training is used in particular when severance costs and labor market frictions are high. To the extent that the time spent in training is paid, added layers of training may act as an opportunity to buy transition time until workers are able to get a job. This effect could be seen during the railway project in Brazil. Workers who took part in the project were offered two types of training, but most found a job without completing the more specialized training (Estache, Schmitt, and Sydenstricker 2000), suggesting that specific training has limited impact in practice.

The training program for the displaced railway employees in Brazil also showed that when offered training options covering a wide range of skills, workers know exactly what they want and how to get trained to improve their chances of finding a job. In the railway project in Brazil, the majority of workers self-selected to participate in general training on how to run a business (Estache, Schmitt, and Sydenstricker 2000). Similar outcomes were illustrated by Loewenstein and Spletzer (1999) for U.S. workers. Data from Ireland confirm that general training raises productivity, but the same cannot be said about specialized training (Estache, Schmitt, and Sydenstricker 2000).

Overall, the main message of this literature is that if the goal of subsidized jobs is to provide support for inclusion in the job market, the design of training needs to be part of the design of the job creation program. Specific training should be considered only if there is market demand for these skills or if there is a need to buy time in a labor market restructuring transition. Often, general training supporting labor market flexibility will be sufficient and more efficient in increasing productivity.

Minimizing the Cost of Job Creation Targeting

Different types of job subsidy targeting strategies involve different types of implementation and monitoring costs as well as different degrees of effectiveness (Amin, Das, and Goldstein 2008). There are relatively easy solutions to reduce these costs, but they take time to be put in place. In MENA, vouchers may be considered to reduce the costs of targeting as they are more efficient than direct subsidies, and targeting the long-term unemployed is more efficient than the less qualified (Brown, Merkl, and Snower 2011).

The design of targeting practices is essential to the effectiveness of the program. When targeting is not direct, firms will potentially select beneficiaries that would have been more likely to find a job without the transfer policy (Marx 2001). This increases the risk of deadweight loss through substitution effects. There is also a risk that, if the measures have not been designed to target a sufficiently large range of potential beneficiaries, some employers will not take the time and energy to use them. Finally, the real risk is that only large and public firms will benefit from these programs because these firms have the capacity to mobilize the resources needed to capture the subsidies. There is thus a tradeoff between the fact that generous measures generate a greater response but also a greater burden.[1]

One way to avoid the risks and costs of direct targeting is to design subsidies such that workers self-select for the subsidized jobs. The objective of self-targeting policies is to ensure that certain categories of workers, poor people or women for instance, self-select into the subsidized jobs, whereas the nontargeted groups choose regular jobs. The subsidies must therefore be such that targeted workers are willing to accept the job (participation constraint) and do not have a better job opportunity (incentive compatibility). Similarly, incentive compatibility must be such that nontargeted groups refuse the subsidized jobs. However, if the resulting wage is too low, this self-targeting subsidy can tend precisely to emphasize the wage gaps and stigmatize a category of workers (Devereux and Solomon 2006).

Is Subsidizing Job Creation a Sustainable Policy?

When considering the option of subsidizing the creation of jobs, governments invariably face the challenge of determining the optimal duration of subsidizing infrastructure. In case of a temporary economic downturn, short-term wage subsidies are a good option to avoid hysteresis. A short-term policy of wage subsidies increases the probability of beneficiaries being employed (Bell and Orr 1994; Betcherman, Daysal, and Pages 2010; Forslund, Johansson, and Lindqvist 2004; Kangasharju 2007; Katz 1996; Marx 2001; Sianesi 2002). However, there is a deadweight loss of subsidizing jobs that can be quite significant. The main risk comes from substitution effects, which can lead to some categories of workers being priced out of the market by subsidized ones. One of the main challenges is therefore to ensure that the subsidized jobs are actually "new" jobs. It has been documented that when firms are required to certify that they have created new jobs, the deadweight loss can be lower (Marx 2001; Kangasharju 2007).

However, the costs associated with the failure to get it right are high. Comparing two programs for Turkey, Betcherman, Daysal, and Pages (2010) found that, for one of the programs, between 47 and 78 percent of the subsidized jobs would have been created without the subsidy. In the second one, the efficiency was higher, and they found that between 23 and 44 percent of the subsidized jobs would have been created without the subsidy. The better outcome in the second case can be explained by the fact that under the second law, the job creation objective was more specific and firms had to increase their total employment by at least 20 percent to be eligible for subsidies.[2]

The Turkish result is unfortunately quite representative. An earlier study argued that in various other countries, leakages of this type were estimated to be above 66 percent (OECD 1993).[3] In the United States, Bishop and Montgomery (1993) showed that for a very general tax credit widely used in the 1990s, at least 70 percent of the credits were estimated to be payments for workers who would have been hired without the subsidy.[4] Martin and Grubb (2001) reviewed various studies and reported that such leakages were up to 90 percent in Australia, Belgium, Ireland, and the Netherlands.

In poor countries, infrastructure subsidies bring an additional concern arising from the potentially perverse incentive that entices people away from agricultural jobs. A way to reduce such a risk could be to support infrastructure in the off-season for farming. The impact of short-term infrastructure subsidies could also lead to competition for workers from other sectors and an upward pressure on wages, with potentially negative consequences for competitiveness. The poverty reduction impact of such higher wages is also questionable, as they may not translate into higher buying power because the prices of key goods and services consumed by the poor could increase as well. Targeting of short-term, relatively specialized, infrastructure jobs may reduce substitution effects. However, if the wage elasticity is lower in the sector, total job creation from a given short-term budget may end up being lower than hoped for (Bucher 2010; Gerfin, Lechner, and Steiger 2005; Sianesi 2002).

Long-term subsidized programs are typically considered in response to mass layoffs from a major economic restructuring. The main challenge in these cases is to avoid sustaining sectors or activities, which have no prospects for future development (ILO/IMF 2010). In the case of infrastructure, subsidized work programs can contribute two types of jobs: (1) those that support the investment components of the sector (known as CAPEX) in the short term and (2) long-lasting jobs created to operate and maintain the long-lived assets (these expenditures are known as OPEX) in the industry.

When committing to support jobs over a longer period of time, the risk of generating perverse incentives would potentially increase as there might be a notion that subsidies would be permanent. One such perverse incentive is the effect long-term wage subsidies have on displacement costs, that is, job losses in nonsubsidized firms through distortion of competition (Marx 2001). Also, if job subsidies permit people to enjoy generous unemployment benefits, people might switch from relying on benefits to relying on subsidized jobs instead of entering the labor market (Sianesi 2002), and some categories of workers might be locked in temporary and subsidized jobs (Van Ours 2004).

There are some positive aspects too. Subsidies can compensate for the implicit tax on severance imposed by employment protection and avoid displacement costs, if the value of the subsidy is higher than severance costs (Galasso, Ravallion, and Salvia 2004; Mortensen and Pissarides 2003). Experience from Finland shows that no displacement costs were observed because subsidized jobs had to be new and only one-third of the wage was being subsidized (Kangasharju 2007). Finally, it is important to keep in mind that long-term programs can be seen as a redistribution device (Brown, Merkl, and Snower 2011), but that the odds of generating a lot of perverse incentives in the process are quite high.

In sum, short-term subsidized work programs can be used more efficiently than long-term programs to facilitate inclusion in the labor market. Wage subsidies in infrastructure works can be designed to limit perverse incentives but to do so a serious diagnosis of the local labor market characteristics is required.

What Are the Net Fiscal Costs and Benefits of Job Creation Programs?

Infrastructure investments also have macroeconomic implications beyond questions related to incentives and efficiency. These include the aggregate fiscal effects of employment subsidy programs and the identification of added costs and benefits associated with these programs.

One of the biggest benefits of infrastructure employment programs is the reduction in income transfers needed and the increased formalization of the economy. Wage subsidies reduce income transfer payments by the government through increases in employment (Bell and Orr 1994). Employment creation programs are also often described as a cost-effective way of providing social protection to the poor (Devereux and Solomon 2006). However, it is not clear how much of a tax benefit such policies represent if many of the jobs created are low skilled and low taxed. Ultimately, the dominant effect of subsidies can be to increase social security registration of firms and workers rather than boosting total employment and economic activity and taxes, as was found by Betcherman, Daysal, and Pages (2010) for Turkey and Galasso, Ravallion, and Salvia (2004) for Argentina.

From a fiscal point of view, there are many potential sources of cost inefficiency. First, in addition to the direct fiscal cost of providing the subsidies, as identified in the previous sections, there are also costs like (1) the deadweight loss of taxation; (2) the cost of demonstration and training services; and (3) the management costs associated with the costs of reaching and informing local employers—costs that are usually hidden in regular government administration. The latter can be significant as the perceived complexity and administrative costs can be a disincentive for potential employers to use the schemes. Systems based on vouchers are usually considered the most efficient, as they significantly reduce the administrative costs for small businesses (Marx 2001). Some studies argue that they can be designed as self-financing tools (Brown, Merkl, and Snower 2011).

Second, costs depend on a number of factors. The first factor is particularly important for large infrastructure projects and relates to the mix of locals and expatriates involved in program design and implementation. The second factor is the choice of delivery mechanism and relates to the design of procurement rules, that is, the modalities of hiring private contractors; the wage-rate-setting process; the capital intensity of operations; the cost of nonlabor inputs; the costs of training provision; and the administrative capacity and its costs.

Finally, there are more subtle cost drivers that can be quite relevant in the decision to allocate large fiscal resources to support job creation. These include the opportunity cost of government spending in the context of limited fiscal capacity; the quality of the institutions, including the ability to coordinate programs linked to various government levels and agencies within government; the risk of benefit capture by local elites and pressure groups; and biased allocation of public resources for political purposes (Devereux and Solomon 2006).

Recent history shows that in MENA these are not minor risks. The associated fiscal costs are high in many countries, but they may be minor compared to the political costs, especially those related to effective coordination between central, regional, and local levels. Such coordination is vital but problems arise when there are inadequate links between the different tiers of government.

Overall, it is difficult to predict the short- and long-term fiscal effects of public infrastructure job programs. They depend on the extent to which wage subsidies increase the formalization of the labor market, the impact this formalization has on public revenue and expenditure obligations, and a large number of indirect and often underestimated costs associated with these employment support mechanisms. When considering the real costs of subsidies, one has to take into account the fiscal capacity of the government, the efficiency of the administrative process, and the risk of corruption and capture. A recent report on investment in MENA (World Bank 2011) shows that in economies with weak rule of law, there is no evidence that public investment stimulates private investment and growth. In contrast, in countries with an adequate level of property rights' protection, accountability, and legal institutions, public investment is strongly linked to growth. In addition, good rule of law helps attract private investment and countries with good rule of law show higher levels of investment efficiency.

Concluding Remarks

This study assesses the potential for job creation through infrastructure investment in the MENA region. The need to achieve tangible employment results relatively quickly has become an urgent need in the context of the Arab Spring events. Moreover, heightened regional and global uncertainty has temporarily restrained private investment, the traditional source of new jobs in expanding economies.

It is well known that, if effectively directed and fostered, infrastructure investment has deep and far-reaching impact on economic and social development. Infrastructure projects can serve as a potential source of immediate jobs and can boost long-term growth and employment through associated gains in productivity. The social payoff of developing sustainable and integrated basic infrastructure is also significant. Improved provision of high-quality basic infrastructure services, such as hospitals, schools, and water supply and sanitation, raises living standards, and enhances employability of populations and prospects for inclusive growth.

MENA countries have been investing in infrastructure over the years. Both in the 1990s and 2000s, public investment spending in MENA was higher than in most developing regions, largely because of robust spending in the oil exporting countries, which benefited from rising fuel prices. Spending on infrastructure boosted employment in the construction sector, which was a major source of job growth in the 2000s relative to other sectors and other countries. Maintaining momentum in infrastructure spending will be important to keep growth and job creation from receding.

Although the infrastructure investment in the overall region on the whole has been strong, there is wide variation across countries in the quality and quantity of infrastructure. The Gulf Cooperation Council (GCC) group has the best infrastructure endowments and services in the region, reflecting high-income levels and commitment to infrastructure investments financed by oil revenues. However, infrastructure deficiencies in developing MENA economies remain a concern. Public investment spending has been particularly weak in the OICs, which have much more limited fiscal space than the oil exporting countries. Although public investment rates increased in the oil exporting countries in the 2000s relative to the 1990s, the opposite happened in the OICs. Recent growth in public-private partnerships was beginning to fill the gap in some OICs, but the economic consequences of the Arab uprisings, combined with economic difficulties in Europe, have strained fiscal budgets in developing MENA economies and reduced private investment, with possible negative consequences for infrastructure spending. Furthermore, gaps are likely to magnify as demand for infrastructure grows with population and income growth, and as countries tackle challenges related to water and energy conservation, efficiency, and climate change.

This study estimates MENA's infrastructure investment and maintenance needs through 2020 at US$106 billion per year or 6.9 percent of the annual regional gross domestic product (GDP). OECs will need to commit almost 11 percent of their GDP annually ($48 billion) on improving and maintaining their national infrastructure endowments, whereas the OICs and the GCC oil exporters need approximately 6 and 5 percent of their GDP, respectively. Investment and rehabilitation needs are especially high in the electricity and transport sectors, particularly roads. Rehabilitation needs will account for slightly more than half of the total infrastructure needs.

While oil exporting countries will be able to meet their national infrastructure needs if they maintain investment spending at the rates prevailing in the 2000s, OICs will fall short. As the vast majority of funding for infrastructure comes from public budgets, it will be critical to protect public investment budgets and try to increase resources going to the sector, especially in the case of OICs. Doing so will be a smart choice for governments looking to create jobs and growth.

MENA's infrastructure sectors, including construction and infrastructure services, employ close to one-fifth of the regional workforce or 18.2 million people. About 10.6 million workers are employed in construction, whereas the remaining 7.6 million provide infrastructure services, but there are significant variations across countries. Within infrastructure services, the transport and communication sectors are the biggest employers, whereas energy and water represent a small fraction of infrastructure workers.

In addition to being a large employer, infrastructure has the potential to contribute significantly to employment creation in MENA. In the short-run, every US$1 billion invested in infrastructure has the potential of generating, on average, around 110,000 infrastructure-related jobs in the OICs, 49,000 jobs in the OECs, and 26,000 jobs in the GCC economies. The region could therefore generate 2.5 million infrastructure-related jobs just by meeting estimated, annual investment needs, but the potential varies greatly across countries. Put differently, these jobs would never materialize if countries instead decide to trim their public investment rates going forward.

Because of per capita income differences, the spending of US$1 billion generates more than six times as many jobs in a sector in low-income Djibouti than in upper middle-income Lebanon, but the latter would find it easier to finance this investment expenditure. Spending on construction of roads and bridges would generate more jobs as the same amount of spending in any other infrastructure sector. This is because the cost of an infrastructure job in the roads and bridge construction sector is about one-fifth of the cost of a job in the electricity-generating sector, and slightly less than one-tenth of the cost of a job in the transport and communication services sector. However, sectors differ in their propensity to generate indirect jobs. It depends on the extent to which the sector requires inputs from other sectors to produce its output. This indicates that when investment decisions are made with the objective of creating jobs, consideration should be given to both direct and indirect employment effects as well as the type of skills required to implement projects.

The long-term employment effect of infrastructure investment could be significant. The study finds that the employment response induced by infrastructure investment resulting in 1 percentage point additional growth is expected to be 9 million additional jobs in the course of 10 years in MENA or a little less than 1 million jobs per year. Such a response is significant as it accounts for approximately 30 percent of the jobs created in the region during the 2000s. Had these jobs been created during the last decade, the unemployment rate would have been substantially lower than the 10 percent registered in 2009.

A switch to labor-intensive technology could enhance the employment creation effect of infrastructure investment, and it may also reduce overall costs. The report discusses the possibility of doing so in the maintenance of unpaved roads and finds that the use of labor-intensive technology reduces investment needs in the region by 0.3 percent of GDP. But solely focusing on costs is probably not the best criterion when considering labor-intensive technologies. The cost structure of labor-intensive infrastructure provision is different from equipment-intensive alternatives, as it includes components like training or development of institutional capacity. Direct comparisons of labor versus nonlabor costs can therefore be misleading.

Prudent infrastructure development will be critical for short- and long-term growth and job creation, as the greatest risk to using infrastructure as part of an employment and growth strategy in the MENA countries is poor governance. Not all jobs are equal, so investments in infrastructure will need to be prioritized based on the employment and infrastructure needs of the country. For example, road and bridge construction projects will have a direct impact on the creation of relatively low-skilled jobs. These types of projects will be especially effective in addressing job-related concerns in countries where there is a large pool of relatively unskilled and unemployed nationals. This is the case in most MENA countries where the majority of the unemployed do not have tertiary education. By contrast, projects in transport and communication services have large indirect effects and, therefore, the ability to create a diverse set of jobs for workers with different skill levels. These projects will appeal to policy makers in countries where the unemployed have the ability to acquire specialized skills relatively quickly.

Public works and different types of subsidized employment programs have been used widely to make it easier for people who cannot find unsubsidized jobs to find employment and acquire on-the-job skills. Traditionally, subsidized employment programs in infrastructure and construction have been used to create employment opportunities for low-skilled workers. But, subsidized employment programs are costly and should be designed to ensure that there is a positive spillover to long-run employment and employability. Experience shows that the latter can be accomplished only if subsidized employment programs are combined with training and counseling.

Infrastructure investments could provide a quick response and be part of the solution to MENA's unemployment challenge, but infrastructure alone will not resolve this problem. Countries should proceed with reforms that improve the business environment, especially business regulations and governance. The literature underscores the importance of a sound regulatory environment and good governance for inclusive growth. This study focused on estimating the employment impact of infrastructure investment in MENA. In the future, more work needs to be done to assess the impact of infrastructure investment on different types of labor, for example, skilled versus unskilled, young versus old, and domestic versus migrant workers.

Notes

1. We assume that (1) equal incremental increases in taxes lead to progressively larger welfare losses and (2) equal incremental increases in each employment subsidy leads to progressively smaller incremental increases in employment and social welfare, and a progressively larger government budgetary outlay (Brown, Merkl, and Snower 2011).

2. The authors compared regions eligible for the subsidies (the "treatment" group) to regions not eligible (the "control" group). Two types of subsidies were implemented with different regulations.

3. The authors reviewed a study in Ireland, based on employer interviews, and Australia, based on interviews with participants in the program—unemployed workers and employees.

4. This study is based on survey data taken from employers and may therefore even be underestimating the deadweight loss.

References

Amin, S., J. Das, and M. Goldstein. 2008. *Are You Being Served? New Tools for Measuring Service Delivery*. Washington, DC: World Bank.

Bell, S., and L. Orr. 1994. "Is Subsidized Employment Cost Effective for Welfare Recipients? Experimental Evidence from Seven States." *The Journal of Human Resources* 29 (1): 42–61.

Betcherman, G., N. Daysal, and C. Pages. 2010. "Do Employment Subsidies Work? Evidence from Regionally Targeted Subsidies in Turkey." *Labour Economics* 17 (4): 710–22.

Bishop, J., and M. Montgomery. 1993. "Does the Targeted Jobs Tax Credit Create Jobs at Subsidized Firms?" *Industrial Relations: A Journal of Economy and Society* 32 (3): 289–306.

Boeri, T. 1997. "Labour Market Reforms in Transition Economies." *Oxford Review of Economic Policy* 13 (2): 126–40.

Brown, A., C. Merkl, and D. Snower. 2011. "Comparing the Effectiveness of Employment Subsidies." *Labour Economics* 18 (2): 168–79.

Bucher, A. 2010. "Impacts of Hiring Subsidies Targeted at the Long-Term Unemployed on the Low-Skilled Labor Market: The French Experience." *Economic Modelling* 27 (2): 553–65.

Burtless, G. 1985. "Are Targeted Wage Subsidies Harmful? Evidence from a Wage Voucher Experiment." *Industrial and Labor Relations Review* 39 (1): 105–14.

Devereux, S., and C. Solomon. 2006. "Employment Creation Programmes: The International Experience." Issues in Employment and Poverty Discussion Paper 24, Economic and Labour Market Analysis Department, International Labour Organization, Geneva.

Estache, A., J. Schmitt, and E. Sydenstricker. 2000. "Labor Redundancy, Retraining and Outplacement During Privatization: The Experience of Brazil's Federal Railway." World Bank Institute Working Paper, World Bank, Washington, DC.

Forslund, A., P. Johansson, and L. Lindqvist. 2004: "Employment Subsidies: A Fast Lane from Unemployment to Work?" Working Paper 2004:18, Institute for Labour Policy Evaluation, Uppsala.

Gagliarducci, S. 2005. "The Dynamics of Repeated Temporary Jobs." *Labor Economics* 12 (4): 429–48.

Galasso, E., M. Ravallion, and A. Salvia. 2004. "Assisting the Transition from Workfare to Work: A Randomized Experiment." *Industrial and Labor Relations Review* 58 (1): Article 6.

Gerfin, M., M. Lechner, and H. Steiger. 2005. "Does Subsidised Temporary Employment Get the Unemployed Back to Work? An Econometric Analysis of Two Different Schemes." *Labour Economics* 12 (6): 807–35.

ILO/IMF (International Labour Organization/International Monetary Fund). 2010. *"The Challenges of Growth, Employment and Social Cohesion,"* Joint ILO-IMF conference in cooperation with the Office of the Prime Minister of Norway, discussion document, Oslo, Norway, September.

Kangasharju, A. 2007. "Do Wage Subsidies Increase Employment in Subsidized Firms?" *Economica* 74 (293): 51–67.

Katz, L. 1996. "Wage Subsidies for the Disadvantaged." Working Paper 5679, National Bureau of Economic Research, Cambridge, MA.

Loewenstein, M., and J. Spletzer. 1999. "General and Specific Training: Evidence and Implications." *The Journal of Human Resources* 34 (4): 710–33.

Martin, J., and D. Grubb. 2001. "What Works and for Whom: A Review of OECD Countries' Experiences with Active Labour Market Policies." *Swedish Economic Policy Review* 8 (2): 9–56.

Marx, I. 2001. "Job Subsidies and Cuts in Employers' Social Security Contributions: The Verdict of Empirical Evaluation Studies." *International Labour Review* 140 (1): 69–83.

McCord, A., and D. van Seventer. 2004. "The Economy-Wide Impacts of the Labour Intensification of Infrastructure Expenditure in South Africa." SALDRU/CSSR Working Paper 93, Southern Africa Labour and Development Research Unit, University of Cape Town, South Africa.

Mortensen, D., and C. Pissarides. 2003. "Taxes, Subsidies and Equilibrium Labor Market Outcomes." In *Designing Inclusion: Tools to Raise Low-End Pay and Employment in Private Enterprise,* ed. Edmund S. Phelps, 44–73. Cambridge, U.K.: Cambridge University Press.

OECD (Organisation for Economic Co-operation and Development). 1993. *Employment Outlook.* Paris: OECD.

Oskamp, F., and D. Snower. 2006. "The Effect of Low-Wage Subsidies on Skills and Employment." Kiel Working Paper 1292, Kiel Institute for the World Economy, Kiel, Germany.

Rama, M. 2003. "Globalization and Workers in Developing Countries." Policy Research Working Paper 2958, World Bank, Washington, DC.

Richardson, J. 1998. "Do Wage Subsidies Enhance Employability? Evidence from Australian Youth." Centre for Economic Performance Discussion Paper 387, London School of Economics and Political Science, London.

Sianesi, B. 2002. "Swedish Active Labour Market Programmes in the 1990s: Overall Effectiveness and Differential Performance." Working Paper W02/03, Institute for Fiscal Studies, London.

Van Ours, J. 2004. "The Locking-In Effect of Subsidized Jobs." *Journal of Comparative Economics* 32 (1): 37–55.

Wasmer, E. 2006. "General versus Specific Skills in Labor Markets with Search Frictions and Firing Costs." *American Economic Review* 96 (3): 811–31.

World Bank. 2011. *Economic Developments and Prospects Report, Middle East and North Africa: Investing for Growth and Jobs*. Washington, DC: World Bank. http://siteresources.worldbank.org/INTMENA/Resources/World_Bank_MENA_Economic_Developments_Prospects_Sept2011.pdf.